C0-AYF-593

THE BRAIN DRAIN:

Determinants, Measurement and Welfare Effects

THE BRAIN DRAIN

Determinants, Measurement and Welfare Effects

Herbert G. Grubel

Anthony Scott

Grubel, Herbert G., 1934-
The brain drain

Bibliography: p.
ISBN 0-88920-037-8 bd.   ISBN 0-88920-036-X pa.

1. Brain drain - Canada. 2. Brain drain - United States. I. Scott, Anthony, 1923- II. Title.

HD8038.C2G78   331.1'27'0971   C77-001118-7

Wilfrid Laurier University Press
Waterloo, Ontario, Canada

ACKNOWLEDGEMENTS

Most of the chapters herein have been published or presented at conferences. We gratefully acknowledge permission to republish papers originally published and copyrighted as follows:

"The International Flow of Human Capital," *American Economic Review* (May 1966); "The Characteristics of Foreigners in the U.S. Economics Profession," *American Economic Review* (March 1967); "The International Circulation of Human Capital," *Minerva* (Autumn 1967); "Immigration of Scientists and Engineers to the United States," *Journal of Political Economy* 74, 4 (1966); "The Cost of U.S. College Exchange Programs," *Journal of Human Resources* 1, 2 (Fall 1966); "The International Movement of Human Capital: Canadian Economists," *The Canadian Journal of Economics* 2, 3 (August 1969); "The Brain Drain—Is a Human Capital Approach Justified," in W. Lee Hansen, ed., *Education, Income and Human Capital*, National Bureau of Economic Research, 1970; "Determinants of Migration: The Highly Skilled," *International Migration Quarterly Review* 5, 2 (1967). One paper, *Characteristics of Foreign Born and Educated Scientists in the United States,* was written with the help of the National Science Foundation, and uses their data.

This book has been published with the help of a grant from the Social Science Research Council of Canada, using funds provided by the Canada Council.

TABLE OF CONTENTS

PART III
POLICY STUDY

LIST OF TABLES

LIST OF FIGURES

PREFACE

This book brings together the most important papers on the brain drain we have published, either jointly or alone, during the period 1966 to 1970. The theoretical Chapters 3 and 4 have not been published before. They contain the rigorous analysis of the economics of migration of labor integrated with the theory of human capital and of the welfare implications of the international flow of labor and human capital. Our most widely cited paper, "The International Flow of Human Capital," *American Economic Review, Papers and Proceedings*, March 1967, represents a brief summary of these two chapters.

We first became interested in the subject of this book when we were both economists on the faculty of the University of Chicago and our colleague Harry G. Johnson circulated his paper "The Economics of the Brain Drain: The Canadian Case," published in *Minerva*, Spring 1965, which outlined what since has become known as the internationalist approach to the issues raised by the international migration of highly skilled manpower. As the director of a Rockefeller Foundation research project in international economics, H. G. Johnson subsequently assisted us financially in the execution of several empirical studies. Chapters 8 and 9 are based on work which H. Grubel carried out with the support of the National Science Foundation. A. Scott acknowledges the support he received from the University of British Columbia Research Fund and the Canada Council.

During the course of our studies we have had the able assistance of L. Brown, K. Fadner, G. Fulton and C. Poole. Useful Comments on manuscripts were made by M. J. Bowman, H. G. Johnson, C. V. Kidd, R. G. Myers, G. Rosenbluth, T. W. Schultz and J. Vanderkamp.

In preparing this book we tried to integrate the previously published papers into a continuous whole. In so doing we have broken up some papers and drastically shortened others while inserting many pages of transitional text. The papers subjected to this process and the journals in which they have been published previously are: "The Reduction of the Brain Drain: Problems and Policies," *Minerva*; "Determinants of Migration: The Highly Skilled," *International Migration Quarterly Review*; "The Immigration of Scientists and Engineers to the United States," *Journal of Political Economy; Characteristics of Foreign Born and Educated Scientists in the United States, 1966*, National Science Foundation, Office of Manpower Studies, Washington, D.C., 1968; "Countries of Birth of Foreign Born U.S. Scientists, 1966" to be published in the Proceedings of the 1968 Cornell Conference on Human Mobility, G. McGinnis, editor; "The Cost of U.S. College Student Exchange Programs," *Journal of Human Resources*; "The International Migrations of Canadian Economists," *Canadian Journal of Economics*; "The Human Capital Approach to International Migration" published in 1970 by the National Bureau for Economic Research, New York, in a volume edited by Lee Hansen. We thank the publishers of these journals and books for the right to use this material.

In the theoretical part of the book we conclude that the most important welfare effects of migration on the remaining population work through short-run adjustment costs, losses of consumer surplus, government activities and externalities. Unfortunately we were unable to produce empirical estimates of these theoretically most relevant magnitudes. Instead we were forced, like so many other social scientists, by the availability of data into measuring magnitudes whose relevance to the theory and the policy questions is much less strong and direct. We nevertheless hope that the estimates of the number of migrants, stocks of U.S. scientists of foreign birth and the value of international flows of human capital will be useful, if only as an accounting record of recent events which serve as the starting point of rational discussions about the causes and effects of the brain drain and about policies to deal with it.

Since this manuscript has been prepared and its publication in 1977, the brain drain has disappeared almost completely as an issue of public policy discussion in newspapers and by the general public in Europe and North America. Western European countries and the Organization for Economic Cooperation and Development terminated major research studies and attempts to formulate comprehensive policy stands towards the brain drain, largely because the flow of highly skilled people from Western Europe to the United States had become a mere trickle, and in some cases had become a net reverse flow. These changes had occurred at the same time that the U.S. space research and military expenditures were decreased and the image of the United States was tarnished by the Vietnam fiasco and domestic political turmoil.

However, in developing countries, primarily India, and international organizations in which developing countries have an important voice, the brain drain has remained an issue. In 1973 the U.N. General Assembly requested that the Secretary General prepare a report on how the world could deal with the problem.[1] In 1974 UNCTAD in Geneva issued a report dramatizing the magnitude of continuing brain drain flows from developing countries.[2]

At the same time, several scholarly and quasi-public studies of the brain drain, which were started during the 1960s were published and provided some useful insights. At the end of Chapter 1 of this book, we consider the most important results published in two Swedish studies[3] and

[1]United Nations, Report of the Secretary General, "Outflow of Trained Personnel From Developing to Developed Countries," E/C. 8/21 (New York, 1974).

[2]United Nations Conference on Trade and Development, "The Reverse Transfer of Technology: Economic Effects of the Outflow of Trained Personnel from Developing Countries" (Geneva: UNCTAD Trade and Development Board, July 15, 1974) GE74-45088 (mimeo).

[3]Göran Friborg, "A First Preliminary Report Concerning an Investigation by the Commit-

an OECD Report.[4] A U.S. Congressional Staff Study[5] contains a useful review of accumulated knowledge and references to recent publications not found in the bibliography appended to this book. In the Spring of 1974, J. Bhagwati of the Massachusetts Institute of Technology, with the help of the Rockefeller Foundation revived some scholarly interest in the brain drain at a conference in Bellagio, Italy.

The Bellagio Conference dealt with two issues, a proposal for the taxation of brain drain migrants from developing countries by industrial countries' governments and the effect emigration has on the incentive and salary structure of the highly skilled professions in developing countries. The conference resulted in some publications[6] and at the end of Chapter 1 we present our views on the issues raised at the Bellagio Conference.

One high point of the scholarly literature relevant to a study of the brain drain in recent years not considered in the body of this book is the work by G. Psacharopoulos.[7] This book is concerned primarily with a review of the global body of knowledge on human capital which is only indirectly relevant to an economic approach to the brain drain, but it also has some excellent chapters dealing directly with brain drain issues.

A study of the literature on the brain drain which has appeared since the publication of our own writings has convinced us that the present book should continue to be of use to scholars and policy makers. The economic analysis and methodology of measurement employed in our studies remain valid and applicable to future studies. The empirical findings represent an important historic record which may serve as a benchmark for future empirical studies. Our policy conclusions embody the economists' internationalist welfare approach which all other policy discussions can disregard only at the risk of losing credibility.

Vancouver, B.C. *H. G. Grubel*
Spring, 1976 *A. D. Scott*

tee Regarding the Migration of Scientists To and From Sweden" (Stockholm: Swedish Research Council Committee on Research Economics, 1968), Report 20 (mimeo). Göran Friborg, "Brain Drain Statistics: Empirical Evidence and Guidelines" (Stockholm: Swedish Research Council Committee on Research Economics, 1975), Report 6.

[4]Organization for Economic Cooperation and Development, "The Utilization of Highly Qualified Personnel," Venice Conference, 25th to 27th October 1971 (Paris: 1973).

[5]U.S. House of Representatives, Committee on Foreign Affairs, *Brain Drain: A Study of the Persistent Issue of International Scientific Mobility* (Washington: U.S. Government Printing Office, 1974).

[6]*World Development*, Vol. 3, No. 10 (Pergamon Press) and in J. N. Bhagwati and M. Partington, eds., *Taxing the Brain: A Proposal*, Vols. 1 and 2 (Amsterdam: North Holland Publishing Company, 1976).

[7]George Psacharopoulos (with K. Hinchliffe), *Returns to Education: An International Comparison* (Amsterdam: Elsevier Scientific Publishing Company, 1973).

Chapter 1

INTRODUCTION

This book contains a number of studies whose aim it is to provide policy makers with theoretical and empirical information on which future decisions must be based. The studies fall into three logically separable categories. Part I contains theoretical studies, where first a chapter is devoted to analyzing the determinants of migration in general and of highly skilled manpower in particular. Second, two chapters present theoretical models for the analysis of the effects international migration of scientists has on national and per capita incomes and the welfare of the people remaining behind.

Part II contains empirical studies. Several chapters are devoted to presenting and analyzing available statistics on the number of foreign-born scientists in the United States. One chapter presents some calculations of the human capital balance between the United States and the rest of the world resulting from the existence of foreign student programs. Lastly, the book closes with a critical analysis of government policies proposed to end the brain drain.

This book is not concerned with the analysis of problems stemming from the international circulation of highly skilled people on technical missions for private business or public agencies, such as managers, engineers, scholars, and technical experts, or in the Peace Corps. These highly skilled persons provide "services" like those of shipping or insurance which, at least in principle, are measured in official statistics of international payments balances, and affect the foreign exchange markets. In contrast, the concern of this book is with the international migration of human capital, skills and expertise, embodied in persons. Owing to the special nature of human capital, this "traffic" does not show up in foreign exchange markets or balance of payments statistics. The concept of human capital, the problems arising from the need to distinguish brain drain and general migrants on the one hand and migrants and temporary visitors on the other will be discussed at some length in chapters to follow.

Academic writings on the brain drain problem have been surprisingly rare. For example, Brinley Thomas' excellent conference volume on international migration[1] contained papers mentioning the skills and education of immigrants, but almost no reference to the special problem of the emigration of scientists, professionals and other highly qualified persons. The recognition of this special problem has been delayed, in our opinion, by the fact that the international flow of intellectuals has been, in most

[1] Brinley Thomas, ed., *Economics of International Migration* (London: Macmillan, 1958).

decades, overshadowed by general waves of migration representing voluntary exile from political and religious developments and involuntary flight from persecution. Underlying the waves of Jewish, White-Russian, Hungarian, Polish, Irish, Baltic refugee and emigré intellectuals, however, was a steady stream of trained people from the United Kingdom, Scandinavia, the Low Countries, Spain, Portugal, France and Italy to the newly opened lands in the various nineteenth century empires, Latin America and, especially, the United States. These migrations, moreover, were often only the beginning—the same people or their children moved on to better prospects, sometimes again as refugees, but more often as a new "upper-class" of migrants soon to be assimilated among the professionals of their newest homeland.

Although it was noticed by economic historians, the brain drain problem had received their attention for somewhat different reasons from those which gave rise to this book. The movements of trained workers were regarded as the most important practical means of transmitting information and technology. For example, the geographic transfer of textile technology, like that of printing and publishing, is alleged to have been accomplished by the flight of specialists.[2] That these two industries are believed to have expanded and shifted in this way is important for general economic history, for they are usually said to be among the leaders, or even harbingers, of general economic growth.

Such transmissions of information and technology are today the subject of research by international trade specialists rather than manpower scholars. The latter, apparently overwhelmed by the difficulties of conceptualizing manpower planning in developing societies, usually ignore the outflow of trained personnel, the gain of such personnel from other countries, and the in-and-out-flows of students moving from their homes to schools, and so on, or back to final occupations. It is not surprising, therefore, that the brain drain has emerged as a topic publicized and studied by economists not usually associated with population, migration or scientific policy.[3]

The book *The Brain Drain*, edited by W. Adams and published in 1968, is the only other book dealing directly with the problem of the brain drain. It is a volume reproducing conference papers that, while stimulating, do not reflect much original research. Rather, the authors were, for the most part, content to apply their expertise in other subjects to some policy

[2]Steven Dedijer, "'Modern' Migration," in W. Adams, ed., *The Brain Drain* (New York: Macmillan, 1968), pp. 9-28; W. W. Rostow, *The Stages of Economic Growth* (Cambridge, 1960); Herbert Butterfield, *The Origins of Modern Science* (New York: Macmillan, 1960); and W. C. Dampier, *A Shorter History of Science* (New York: Meridian, 1957).

[3]Frederick Harbison, for example, after some important work on education and manpower planning, has turned to the brain drain. But his earlier volume, C. A. Myers and F. Harbison, *Education, Manpower and Economic Growth* (New York: McGraw-Hill, 1963), neglected the existence of a world open economy in the market for trained personnel.

aspects of this new problem. Consequently, many of the papers lack a sense of perspective which only greater in-depth study of the problem can provide.

On the other hand, the Adams volume does usefully summarize many of the political issues and ventures to recommend reasonable and politically practical policies. For readers who are interested in discovering whether there *is* cause for concern, and whether the problem is large enough to justify massive reform of our present institutions, more knowledge is clearly required. The Adams volume contains a set of studies which raises the relevant questions but does not go far in answering them.

SOME 1976 REFLECTIONS ON THE MEASUREMENT OF THE BRAIN DRAIN[4]

During the 1960s when public concern with the brain drain was at its peak the most readily available, seemingly reliable and comprehensive statistics on the flow of highly skilled persons to the United States were those published by the United States Immigration and Naturalization Service,[5] which also underlay the data published by the United States National Science Foundation.[6] These statistics continue to be quoted uncritically by many analysts and they play a key role in the publications of the United Nations Conference on Trade and Development of 1974[7] and the United States House of Representatives.[8] Yet, these statistics are highly misleading and overstate to a significant degree the gains of the United States and the losses of the rest of the world in migrants and human capital because they do not include information about return-migration or the place where the skilled person received his education. The reasons for this omission are simple. The United States immigration authorities do not keep a record of highly skilled persons leaving the United States and they do not distinguish in their records between persons who were educated in the United States or abroad. Similarly, foreign governments do not record the return of native-born persons who in most countries can re-enter simply by showing their passports.

In order to obtain reliable statistics on return-migration from the United States, investigators in some Western European countries had to engage in an expensive and painstaking search of other records, for example,

[4]The remainder of this chapter is based on H. Grubel, "Reflections on the Present State of the Brain Drain and a Suggested Remedy," *Minerva* (1976). It was written after the author attended the Bellagio Conference on the brain drain and in response to the papers and discussions which took place there.

[5]For an excellent collection of information on data sources for the estimation of brain drain flows, see Friborg, "Brain Drain Statistics: Empirical Evidence and Guidelines"; and OECD, "The Utilization of Highly Qualified Personnel."

[6]National Science Foundation, *Scientists, Engineers, and Physicians from Abroad: Trends through Fiscal Years* (Washington: National Science Foundation), various years.

[7]Ibid.

[8]Ibid.

records of church registration in Sweden, military records in Switzerland, and special computation by the United Kingdom Ministry of Technology in order to obtain information about returned emigrants.[9]

On the basis of these investigations, return migration during the period from 1958 to 1969 accounts for between 40 and 90 per cent of recorded gross migrations.[10] Figure 1.1, taken from an OECD Report, shows the available statistics on gross and net migration for several countries and occupations. As can be seen from the figure, in the case of Dutch engineers, in a two-year period more returned to Holland from the United States than left for the United States. Probably the estimate of immigration into the United States is still overestimated because during the period flows were growing rapidly and people tended to stay a number of years in the United States. To count only inflows and outflows over a given period neglects the emigration of the larger numbers in subsequent years. Even if net immigration were zero, rising gross flows and a stay of several years in the United States would show a net gain for the United States within any given period of time. Many highly skilled Swedish migrants are very mobile internationally, giving rise to what Göran Friborg has called a "yo-yo" effect, meaning that some individuals enter and depart several times within a given period. These in the past have sometimes been counted several times as immigrants, but never as emigrants from the United States. There is every reason to believe that for many of the poorer countries also net flows are much smaller than gross flows.[11]

The magnitude of losses of human capital incurred by emigration of highly skilled persons to the United States is overstated by United States statistics of immigration by the further fact that they do not include the country where the immigrant was educated. The immigration to the United States of a person wholly educated abroad and of a person whose education was undertaken in, and perhaps even paid for by the United States should be treated differently. Despite the deficiency of American statistics on this matter, there are some indirect clues to the relative magnitude of the foreign and American education of immigrants to the United States. In 1970, of the 13,337 scientists and engineers who received immigrant visas, 5,470, or 41.0 per cent were in the United States at the time they had their visas changed from visitor's, student's and other classes of visa.[12] The overwhelming proportion of these changes in type of visa were for students who had received a significant and the most expensive part of their education in the United States. Furthermore, some of the remaining 59.0 per cent received their advanced training in the United States but applied for immigrant status from abroad because of the particular requirements of the

[9]For more details on these studies see the sources cited in footnote 2 of this chapter.

[10]OECD, "The Utilization of Highly Qualified Personnel."

[11]Friborg, "A First Preliminary Report ... Regarding the Migration of Scientists to and from Sweden."

[12]OECD, "The Utilization of Highly Qualified Personnel."

type of visa under which they had entered the United States initially as students. Others received their higher education in another industrial country like Canada, Great Britain, or Western Germany.

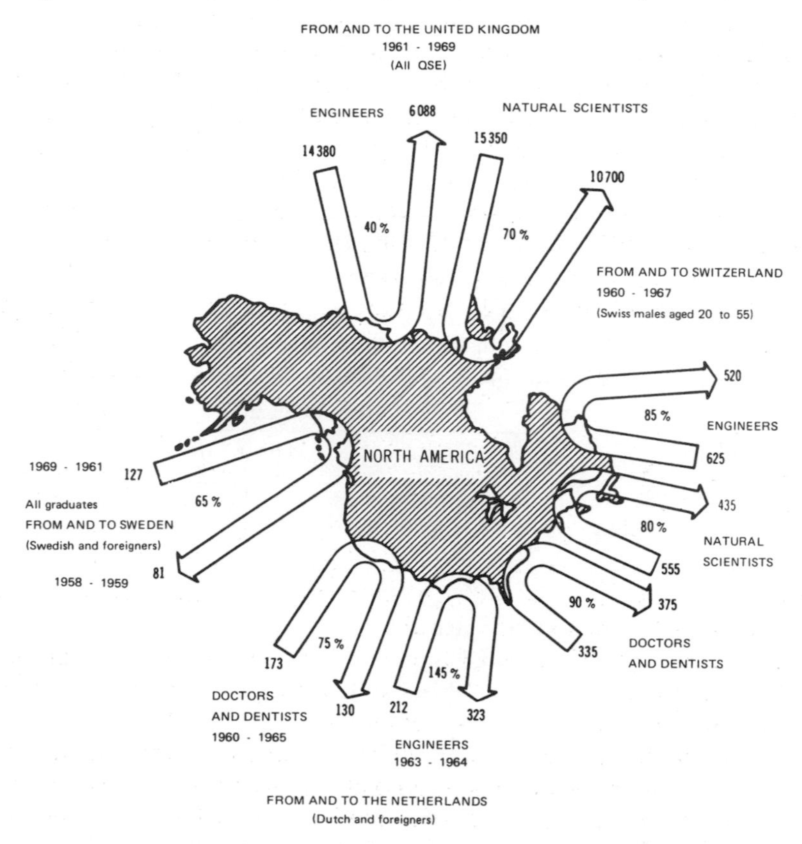

Figure 1.1

Flows of Foreign High Level Scientific and Technical Personnel to and from North America (Selected Countries, Years and Occupations)

With the notable exception of Great Britain and Switzerland, between 30 and 85 per cent of foreign-born holders of doctorates in the United States received at least their final degree in the United States. In the case of the poorer countries in the list, for example, Greece and Turkey, the proportion of doctorates acquired in the United States is above three-quarters.

SOME THOUGHTS ON THE BELLAGIO CONFERENCE AND DISCUSSION

We have already mentioned in the previous section that, in February 1975 a conference of specialists met at the Rockefeller Conference Center in Bellagio, Italy, to discuss the merits of a proposal[13] to impose a tax on highly skilled persons from developing countries who are resident in developed countries. This proposal was considered by the Rockefeller Foundation to be important enough to warrant financing of the conference and it is highly likely that it will receive world-wide attention as a result of the publication of the proceedings of the conference.[14] For this reason, we would like to present some thoughts on the merit of this tax proposal, which matured during the discussions at the Bellagio conference. In so doing, we will consider only the brain drain flows of non-medical personnel to the United States and will disregard the special problems raised by the immigration of doctors and nurses from some poor countries to North America and Britain.

Table 1.1

Place of Doctoral Study of Foreign Born Scientists with Doctorates in the United States in 1966 (%)

	Area of award		
Country	Home country	Other	U.S.A.
United Kingdom	72.5	5.5	22.0
Japan	60.9	1.3	37.0
Germany	60.5	8.1	31.4
Italy	60.4	5.2	34.4
France	30.8	10.0	59.3
Switzerland	76.1	4.0	19.9
Austria	59.8	7.3	32.9
Netherlands	57.9	3.2	38.8
Sweden	58.2	2.3	39.5
Finland	42.2	7.8	50.0
Belgium	35.7	5.3	59.0
Canada	23.7	3.2	73.1
Denmark	34.0	7.4	58.6
Norway	28.8	17.5	53.7
Spain	53.9	11.0	35.1
Yugoslavia	26.8	24.7	48.5
Ireland	21.6	27.4	51.0
Greece	6.8	7.6	85.7
Turkey	5.7	24.3	74.9

Source: Organization for Economic Cooperation and Development, *The Utilization of Highly Qualified Personnel.*

The following discussion about recent trends is based on information gathered by talking to individuals in governments, international organizations and universities, who are in intimate direct contact with the brain

[13]This proposal was first advanced in the article by J. Bhagwati and W. Dellalfar, "The Brain Drain and Income Taxation," *World Development*, 1, 1 and 2 (1973).

[14]Precise references to these publications are contained in footnote 6 of this chapter.

drain problems through their work. As a result, the generalizations to be made are undocumented and should be treated with a certain amount of scepticism. However, at the same time, it is also important to realize that official representations by governments in international organizations, such as the United Nations or UNCTAD, cannot be taken at face value as reflections of the seriousness of the brain drain problem from developing countries. It is well known that such agencies to some extent serve as a forum for ideological pronouncements and efforts by third-world countries to exact income transfers from industrial nations. The issue of the brain drain has much emotional content and lends itself well to the attainment of these objectives. Developing countries have every incentive to exaggerate and none to minimize the seriousness of the brain drain problem.

In a longer perspective, it is obvious that there was an abnormally large flow of highly skilled persons into the United States in the 1960s and that this large flow has now ended. This cycle has been produced by the interaction of many factors. During the 1960s the economy of the United States was expanded greatly and its government embarked on several large-scale scientific and engineering projects simultaneously. These included the program of the exploration of outer space, very large and growing expenditures on basic research in physics, chemistry, and medicine, scientific and engineering expenditures connected with the war in Vietnam and increased support for the expansion of higher education which required many more teachers in many fields. During this period, foreign students came to American universities in vast numbers, some attracted by the prestige and achievements of American science and engineering at the time and by the opportunities for financial support. On graduation, many of these students easily found lucrative employment in the United States.

Since the years of the 1960s, conditions have changed. U.S. government expenditures on space, fundamental and military research have fallen in real terms. University enrollment has ceased to expand and in many fields there are unemployed or underemployed graduates with advanced degrees. The prestige of American science and engineering has lost some of its lustre. Urban disorders have tarnished the image of the United States as a paradise on earth. At the same time, most other countries of the world are enjoying relatively stable economic growth with concomitant opportunities for educated people to find satisfactory employment in their own countries. As a result, the net migration of highly educated persons has been reduced to such an extent that the issue of the brain drain has all but disappeared from public and governmental discussions. European governments, which once were very much concerned about the problem, have used their influence to bring an end to all further research on the topic in the OECD. We have been told by informed sources that there are practically no more representations from Latin American governments to the

United States Department of State as there were during the 1960s. In Asia there appear to be only two countries with persistent brain drain problems, the Phillipines and India. In the former case, a long, traditional tie with the United States has created special conditions and it has been said there that unilateral actions by the United States government to resist the flow of physicians and nurses to the United States would not be welcomed. Such action would in effect amount to the outside interference with a deliberate domestic Phillipine policy of producing more doctors and nurses than are required domestically, in part in order to create the opportunity for some to have a successful career in medical science in the United States. The solution to this problem—if it is a problem—as it is seen by some observers, must be found in the domestic Phillipine policies and it is not the business and even less the responsibility of the United States to intervene in the matter.

As far as India is concerned, many analysts of Indian conditions have concluded that India has overinvested in education since the end of the Second World War and has produced too many university graduates, and as a result a large number of these are seeking employment abroad.[15] Such emigration is economically rational and efficient from the point of view of both the emigrating individual and of his country. If the Indian government considers this brain drain undesirable socially, then it should cease the excess production of highly skilled persons or it should impose controls on emigration. The income tax on emigrants which was proposed by Bhagwati and Dellalfar would reduce the need for the government of India to choose between politically unpopular policies, but it would not deal with the situation of which the brain drain is only a result.

Such a tax would have many costs. It would be difficult to obtain the necessary legislation in the Congress of the United States and it would probably face a test of constitutionality in the Supreme Court, it would be costly and difficult to administer and it would reduce otherwise highly desirable international mobility of highly educated persons and students throughout the world. Very importantly, as Dr. C. Diaz-Alejandro observed during the Bellagio Conference discussion, the existence of such a tax would in principle enable governmental officials to raise the tax rate to such a high level that they could prevent all migration if they considered it to be in the national interest at the moment. Given these costs of the tax for the entire world and the fact that in recent years the problem of the brain drain concerns only a few countries, there must be serious doubts as to the desirability of initiating such a tax.

The Bellagio Conference dealt not only with the practical problem of taxing brain drain migrants, but also devoted considerable time to the discussion of a model of how the brain drain affects the welfare of the

[15] For a documentation of this proposition see M. Blaug, P. R. G. Layard and M. Woodhall, *The Causes of Graduate Unemployment in India* (London: Alain Lane, 1969).

population in countries from which the emigrants leave, even if these migrants tend to be paid their marginal social product and taxation-income-redistribution effects do not exist. This model has become known as the "emulation model" and was first presented in the article by Bhagwati and Dellalfar[16] in which they also advanced the proposal for the tax. Because of the originality and potential use of the emulation model as an argument for the imposition of the tax on migrants, it may be useful to discuss briefly the nature and empirical validity of this model. According to the emulation model the emigration of some highly skilled persons from a country causes costs to be incurred by those who remain as a result of the fact that the opportunity to emigrate and to earn a higher income abroad increases the expected rate of return from higher education for all graduates. It strengthens the hands of university graduates in bargaining for higher salaries on the grounds that unless such higher salaries are paid further large and potentially catastrophic emigration would take place. As a result of such bargaining, the salaries of highly skilled persons in countries "emulating" the foreign salaries are raised. Together with the already higher salary expected from emigration, incentives are created for more persons to seek higher education. The resulting shortage of places at universities are met by the politically popular construction of more universities. The increased supply of university graduates, *ceteris paribus*, further increases emigration, which in turn leads to more emulation and so it goes in a vicious circle of increasing waste and inefficiency. Professors Bhagwati and Dellalfar then conclude that if there had been no brain drain, emulation would not occur and the country which suffers from emulation would not be faced with the waste entailed in the over-production of highly educated persons. The model implies that if the brain drain could be reduced or stopped through some policy such as a tax on emigrants, the social cost of emulation could be lowered or eliminated.

The emulation model is an attractive intellectual construction, but we think that it is unrealistic. In the case of India, historic sequences do not correspond to the emulation model. The salaries of Indian civil servants who had a higher education have been at a disequilibratedly high level, relative to other wages, ever since independence, primarily because the new Government of India simply accepted the structure of remuneration which had been followed by the government in British India.[17] Salaries paid to Indian university graduates made for a high demand for more places in universities and to the rapid expansion of India's universities since the end of the Second World War. The excessive supply of Indian university graduates occurred earlier than the brain drain and caused it. The conflict between these two competing interpretations of the cause of

[16]See footnote 1 of this chapter.

[17]This argument has been made by Blaug, et al., *The Causes of Graduate Unemployment in India*.

the Indian overproduction of university graduates can be resolved only by an empirical test.

Even if one were to accept the Bhagwati-Dellalfar "emulation model" as correct, there is no good reason for thinking that it is in the interest of countries suffering from emulation or any other countries to extend valuable intellectual and political resources on the difficult process of obtaining an international system of taxation. It would be better to try to persuade the public in emulating countries to accept a more realistic view of the supposed benefits of higher education. There is some evidence that economically wasteful processes harming a large segment of a country's population can ultimately be brought under control if they are explained properly and fully discussed in public. Judgments on the relative efficacy of using a given amount of resources for the purpose of instituting a world-wide income tax on migrants or the breaking of emulation processes are difficult to make at best, but a thorough discussion of these issues is needed.

Part I

THEORETICAL STUDIES

Chapter 2

THE DETERMINANTS OF MIGRATION

In this chapter we present a theoretical model of the determinants of migration, paying special attention to the characteristics distinguishing the highly skilled from the general population. This analysis is useful in formulating empirical tests designed to measure the relative importance of various factors entering decisions to migrate or not and ultimately permits the formulation of policies which are aimed at influencing the size and direction of the international migration of highly skilled people.

The behavior of scientists, engineers, artists and intellectuals, the group of people we are calling highly trained, is fundamentally determined by the same kind of motivations and market forces as those of less highly trained workers. We will therefore first present a general theory of the determinants of migration applicable to all people regardless of skill level and will then analyze in what ways the market organization, personality and educational characteristics of the highly trained tend to influence the relative importance of various elements entering their decision-making process.

Throughout the analysis we assume that each decision-making unit, the individual migrant or the family of which he is a part, makes the decision independently from that of any other, and that the basic parameters entering his decision-making process are given to him from the outside and are beyond his influence. The decision-maker furthermore is assumed to act in the full knowledge of all privately relevant consequences of and alternatives to the action. He seeks at all times to maximize the welfare of the unit to which he belongs, which we interpret to mean that he attempts to maximize the present value of net future benefits.

For heuristic reasons we have divided the discussion of the determinants of migration into a section where the migration is once and for all and a section where the migration is potentially reversible. As will be seen, under the more realistic second assumption, the same estimate of the probability of an outcome of an event leads to migration when under the assumptions of irreversibility they would not do so.

DETERMINANTS OF ONCE-AND-FOR-ALL MIGRATION

The parameters entering the decision to migrate once-and-for-all are the expected real income in the country of origin (Y_o) and the country of destination (Y_d) over the expected number of years of life in the respective countries (N_o, N_d); the psychic income in both places (P_o, P_d), which may be negative; the rates of discount applied to the future stream of real income (r_o, r_d) and of psychic income (p_o, p_d); and the cost of moving (C), including earnings foregone during the move and while job hunting.

These parameters enter the individual's calculations in the form shown in the following inequality:

$$\sum_{i=1}^{N_o} \frac{Y_{o,i}}{(1+r_o)^i} + \sum_{i=1}^{N_o} \frac{P_{o,i}}{(1+p_o)^i} \gtreqless \sum_{i=1}^{N_d} \frac{Y_{d,i}}{(1+r_d)^i} + \sum_{i=1}^{N_d} \frac{P_{d,i}}{(1+p_d)^i} - C$$

If a decision-maker's calculations indicate that the right side of the inequality is greater than the left he migrates; in the case of equal values he is indifferent as between staying or leaving; in all other cases he does not migrate.

What is meant by "real income" and "psychic income" is obvious to anyone who has made this type of calculation in connection with his own migration. However, when it comes to giving precise, operational definitions to these concepts, they turn out to be rather complicated.

The comparison of real incomes in two countries normally starts with a conversion of the foreign salary at the existing exchange rate. This procedure, often used in empirical studies, is not very satisfactory for reasons well known from the discussions of the Purchasing Power Parity doctrine. Foremost of these difficulties in the comparison of the value of a certain income converted at an exchange rate is the existence of potentially widely divergent relative prices of commodities. For instance, beef is much more expensive in the United States than in Australia. However, anyone who spends a dollar on meat may derive much more satisfaction in the United States than in Australia if he strongly prefers chicken to beef since chicken is much cheaper in the United States than in Australia. Thus, before being able to arrive at a judgment about the satisfaction one is able to derive from incomes in two places, it is necessary to relate one's own set of tastes to the existing pattern of relative prices.

In addition, one must consider such institutional aspects of living and the employment as length of hours worked, difficulties and cost of commuting between home and place of work, climate, levels of taxation, levels of government services, etc. All of these characteristics affect the total level of satisfaction a man derives from his existence through the command over real resources and leisure. Increased income due to more hours worked is not a net gain. Since one has to get to work and back home one's real income is affected by the availability of public transportation or cheap private means of commuting. Climate determines expenditures for heating and clothing, which may be different between two places and leaves unequal amounts of income for expenditure on other goods and services. The amount of taxes paid and government benefits received may be different in two countries, given a person's position in the life cycle. For instance, a man near retirement may prefer to live in a country with high taxes and high retirement benefits over one where both are low. Upon close inspection it can be seen that in order to arrive at an estimate of the differences in real incomes between two countries an individual has to go through a complicated calculus involving his personal preferences for work, his age and family status in relation to his income, the relative prices of commodities, tax rates, government services, climate and institutional characteristics of the job.

The comparison of psychic incomes between alternative places of residence involves another list of magnitudes which a potential migrant has to examine and weigh in his own mind. The psychic income components have the characteristic that they are non-separable from the environment of the location, cannot be altered by private expenditures and yet influence a person's sense of well-being. Climate, the amount of rainfall and sunshine determines people's happiness in ways which go beyond the expenditures required to keep them dry and have structures with comfortable temperatures. Normally people are not indifferent as to the architecture, natural scenery and vegetation of the area in which they live.

People are similarly influenced in their choice of a country of residence by where in the scale of relative income they find themselves. A man making a real income of $250 per year as a tribal chief in Africa may not be willing to move to the United States for ten times this income, because he would be considered a pauper with an income of only $2,500 a year. Other psychic income items are related to the people with whom one has to associate in the two places of residence. There are costs of giving up the affection of one's family, the association with people of common cultural and historical heritage, and whatever patriotic sentiment is all about. But there may also be gains associated with leaving a personally restricting, though familiar, cultural and social environment.

It is useful to distinguish between psychic elements of the type just listed, which persist past the time of the actual move, and those which are associated with the move itself, such as the discomforts of traveling, learning new customs, skills, language and adjusting to a new environment and the positive gains from the excitement and adventures of travel and moving to a new country. These transitory psychic incomes and costs resemble closely those real costs of moving associated with the transportation of persons and belongings, getting in and out of assets like houses, securities and other real estate and the foregone earnings during travel and search for employment. These two types of costs and benefits are contained in the symbol C in the inequality shown above.

The real and psychic elements entering the decision calculus summarized by the inequality are discounted at the country's market rate of interest or the individual's own rate of discount for psychic income respectively. Such discounting and different rates of interest can be seen to be comparable only by computing the present value of such streams, for clearly the right to $1,000 today and $10,000 ten years from now is not worth as much as the right to the $10,000 today and the $1,000 ten years hence. Given an individual's rate of time preference the level of interest rates prevailing in the alternative place of residence are important, for if he wants to have an equal amount of consumption each year for the next ten years, he can borrow against his future income or lend out his present income, depending on whether the time stream corresponds to the first or second example. The cost of borrowing and the returns from lending at the existing interest thus determine the level of equal annual consumption which the migrant is able to enjoy. Though one cannot lend or borrow psychic costs and benefits in the market, it is reasonable to assume that individuals go through some kind of discounting process with respect to these costs and benefits. There are very few people who consider themselves equally well off in the expectation of having a tooth pulled today and having it pulled ten years from now.

Our model is unrealistic in disregarding the fact that people hardly ever know with certainty what their monetary or psychic incomes will be next month, next year, or any time in the future. The uncertainties surrounding foreign future income and living conditions are even greater than those of the domestic job. A good case can therefore be made for the neglect of discounting adjustments since they are likely to be swamped by the uncertainty for any but the closest periods in the future.

However, people do engage in making estimates of long run future incomes under alternative conditions and they manage to choose among income streams that differ both with respect to the most likely income and the uncertainty that this level will be attained. The theory of portfolio management under uncertainty developed by Markowitz and Tobin[1] has provided us with analytical tools which permit deeper insights into how people choose among assets with different expected rates of return and riskiness about this return. We will apply this same model in slightly modified form to the choice of future incomes, none of which are expected with certainty.

One can carry an experiment and ask people what they think their income next year will be. They will normally give a figure in which they believe with a certain confidence. This confidence can be expressed in terms of probability such as, "I believe that chances are .5 that next year my income will be $5,000." The individual is likely to have further subjective views on the odds that his income will be $4,000, $6,000 or $10,000, etc. The answers thus obtained can be used to make a histogram as shown in Figure 2.1. By smoothing of the discrete steps we arrive at a frequency distribution, the mean of which is the expected income, and the standard deviation of which is a measure for the riskiness associated with the

[1] H. Markowitz, *Portfolio Selection*, Cowles Foundation Monograph 16 (New York: Wiley, 1959). J. Tobin, "Liquidity Preference as Behavior Towards Risk," *Review of Economic Studies* (February 1958).

expected income of his job. Similar experiments can be carried out for other possible opportunities, including some in a foreign country.

We can then put two incomes with their different expected levels and riskiness on a graph as shown in Figure 2.2 and must now develop a criterion which enables us to say which of the two jobs, A or B, is superior. The tool employed in making such an analysis is a quadratic utility function which has expected income and its associated riskiness as arguments. Tobin has developed such a utility function and the resultant indifference curves have approximately the shape of line IoIo in Figure 2.2 for a risk-averter. (See his article, "Liquidity Preference as Behavior Towards Risk," for a mathematical derivation of the indifference curves.) Their essential characteristic for our purpose is that they allow us to show explicitly the kind of trade-off between higher expected income and riskiness that is required to keep a person at the same level of satisfaction. Given the normal assumptions about transitivity there exists a map of non-intersecting indifference curves, those to the north representing higher levels of satisfaction. The indifference curve shown in Figure 2.2 goes through point A and is the highest one attainable given the choice between income A and B. Point B is inferior to A since according to the individual's personal preferences B's higher expected income is insufficient to compensate for the accompanying higher riskiness.

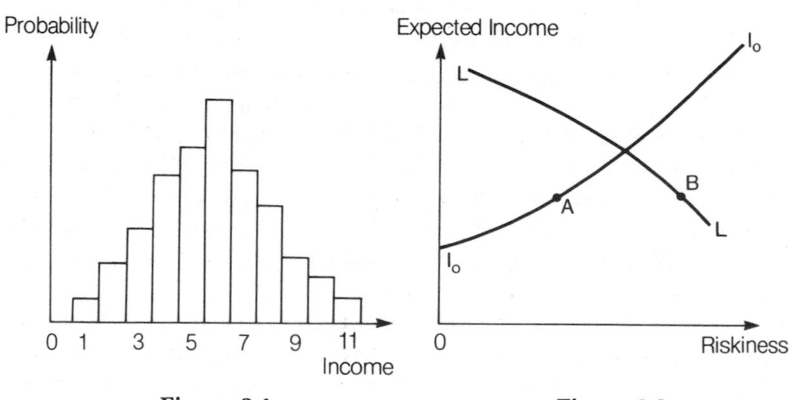

Figure 2.1 **Figure 2.2**

We cannot rule out the possibility that there exist people to whom riskiness is not a disadvantage, but a positive aspect of a job. Simple assumptions about some of the values entering into the specific form of the utility function yield indifference curves shaped like the one labeled LL in Figure 2.2. These people, called risk lovers, will always choose the job with the highest riskiness associated with it. If risk lovers were predominant in job markets, their demand for risky jobs would lower the expected incomes from them and we would expect to observe that jobs with high pay have the low risk. Since observation of job markets shows quite clearly that the opposite is the case there exists a strong presumption that risk averters are predominant over risk lovers.

In the continuation of our experiment we can ask the person to assign a utility value to jobs A and B next year according to their own scale of cardinal utility. We can repeat the entire experiment several times for other years in the future. The result will be a series of expected utility values for each job. For the same reasons that we had to discount income streams known with certainty in order to make them comparable we also have to discount the streams of utility. Presumably such discounting would occur at some personal rate of discount which is not necessarily equal to the market rate of interest.[2]

The entire procedure can be applied to income components other than monetary income just discussed. The model allows us to describe and analyze the factors which enter into individuals' decisions to migrate when none of these factors are known with certainty. This model represents a significant step towards realism over the model where certainty was assumed to exist.

The analysis just completed showed what kind of calculations an individual goes through when he considers migration to one specific country. In addition, some people are likely to engage in the same analysis for several countries and then migrate to the one which brings them the greatest net benefit, if more than one shows an improvement over the alternative of staying at the present residence.

Because of the essential immeasurability of the psychic cost and income items of the decision inequality this model has not been used to predict migratory flows on the disaggregate level. But the model is nevertheless useful in that it identifies those variables which policy makers have to influence if they wish to alter the direction or magnitude of actual flows. Furthermore, the model can be used to measure the relative importance of psychic incomes and costs. L. Sjaastad,[3] in an ingenious study, used actual estimates of income differences and out-of-pocket moving expenses of people who have migrated within the United States and computed from these the implied maximum psychic and other unmeasured costs associated with the move.

Another possible empirical use of our model would be to assume constancy of psychic and moving cost through time and attempt to estimate the income elasticity of aggregate migratory flow.

[2]We choose to discount future utility instead of merely future expected income because it is probable that persons have a myopia (time preference) for future risk as well as for future consumption.

[3]L. Sjaastad, "The Costs and Returns of Human Migration," *Journal of Political Economy*, Part 2, Supplement 70 (1962).

REVERSIBILITY OF MIGRATION AND GENERAL MOBILITY

The model we have just presented implicitly considers migration as a once-and-for-all act, necessitating the evaluation of future streams of income for long periods after the initial decision. Clearly, this aspect of the model is highly unrealistic. In the real world one usually has the opportunity to reconsider the decision to migrate, or to migrate and return home in the light of accumulating new evidence bearing on the decision variables.

It is perhaps intuitively obvious that people's willingness to move is increased if they will be free to move back again at some future date. This willingness can be shown to have two bases. In the first place, if a person has complete certainty about the shape of the time streams of income which he can earn in the two countries, there are many combinations of time shapes imaginable that would induce him to move, earn for a while, then move again, either back home or even to a third country. In medicine, for example, in some countries with private practices, incomes are low in early years but come to a peak in middle age; whereas in countries with socialized medicine incomes may rise very slowly, if at all, over a man's lifetime. If we assume that a doctor's personal efficiency each year is the same regardless of where he practiced last year, then it would pay him to move to a practice in a "welfare state" in his early professional life, and to move again to a private-practice country in later years. Clearly, the profitability of such in-and-out mobility depends upon the income of each period being fairly independent of employment and income in the same country in another period.

In the second place, even when certainty does not exist about the levels of incomes available in the two regions at different dates, probability calculations about events at home and abroad may impel persons to migrate with the possibility of returning later, when in the absence of the opportunity to return they would decide against migrating at all. Assume, for instance, that migration makes possible a new income stream higher than that at home under some circumstances, but lower under others. Given the probability of the second set of circumstances occurring, one should be more willing to migrate and take advantage of higher earnings for a while and return when the conditions are favorable than when the opportunity to return home does not exist.

INDIVIDUAL DECISIONS AND THE AGGREGATE

We have just presented two models where the individual decision-maker was considered to be too small a part of the whole to influence any of the parameter values on the basis of which he made his decision. Now we must relax this assumption, so convenient for purposes of analyzing phenomena on the individual level, and discuss two problems. First, what determines how many migrants are likely to leave during a given time interval and second, how does the system move to a position of equilibrium?

We will in this section continue to speak of migrants in general rather than highly trained individuals since on this level of analysis no essential difference exists between them.

Consider perfect and instantaneous mobility of capital but no international trade in commodities[4] between two countries in the stationary state, i.e., a state without net savings and natural population change. While international capital flows keep the return to capital equal in both countries, we assume that natural conditions, climate, resource endowment, etc., allow the existence of a wage differential between the two countries and a prohibition on migration permits it to persist.

At the moment that the prohibition of migration between the two countries is lifted the size of the income differential, the cost of moving and the psychic income differentials will determine how many people *wish to* migrate in the initial period. We assume that the number of people actually able to migrate has an upper limit determined by the available transportation facilities. Assuming that the number willing to move exceeds the number of places on the transportation facilities we can imagine auctioning off these places to the highest bidders, which guarantees that those people with the highest psychic income from the move are put into the position of obtaining it. The transportation facilities thus determine the size of the flow of migrants during the first period and a market process leads to the selection of individuals.

As a consequence of the flow itself certain changes take place, which reduce the number of people wishing to migrate. According to the law of diminishing returns to variable factors, the wages of remaining workers in the country of emigration will rise and the wages in the country of destination will fall.[5] Thus wage differentials will tend to narrow and, *ceteris paribus*, the incentive to migrate is reduced. This process will continue until no more people wish to migrate.

One can easily imagine ways in which our model of migration can be made more realistic. For instance, the existence of a colony of former migrants in the new country can be assumed to reduce the psychic cost of moving, thus increasing incentives to emigrate. More important, however, would be an extension of the analysis into a world where in both countries population grows, savings are accumulated and technology develops possibly at different rates in the two countries. Such conditions may easily prevent migration ever falling to zero. Basically, however, our conclusion about the aggregate determinants and impact of migration remain: during any given period of time capacity or increasing cost in the use of transportation facilities are likely to limit the flow; over time the flows of labor, *ceteris*

[4]The latter assumption is necessary in order to avoid the possibility of factor price equalization through commodity trade along the lines of the Samuelson factor price equalization theorem.

[5]We will abstract from the flow of capital in the opposite direction induced by this human migration in our model.

paribus, tend to narrow labor-income differentials and reduce incentives to migration.

These models of the determinants of migration are applicable to people of all skill levels, whether they are common laborers, craftsmen, farmers, housewives, or professionals. Yet the concern over the brain drain suggests that there is something special about the international migration of highly skilled individuals. The question therefore arises whether the emigration of these people is proportionately larger than that of all skills or whether certain of their characteristics attract attention so that their departure is more prominently noted. The answer to this question can be found by looking at emigration statistics of countries. But it is also useful to examine the issue on a theoretical level because such considerations are again likely to lead to the identification and better understanding of areas for policy actions aimed at influencing the flow of brainy immigrants.

SPECIAL CHARACTERISTICS OF THE BRAINY MIGRANTS

Absolute Income Differentials

The first difference between migrating laborers and say, engineers, is the existence of a wider absolute gap in earnings. Thus, if an unskilled worker can earn $1,000 and $4,000 in countries A and B respectively, he will increase his earnings by $3,000 by migrating from A to B. Now if in both countries the salaries of engineers are three times those of workers, then an engineer increases his earnings by $9,000 through migration.

If therefore the proportional income differentials in various countries tend to be roughly the same, the greatest absolute gain from migration will go to those who are already well paid, so that migration among such groups should, when a possibility of migrating is open, be greater than among laborers.

But this emphasis on absolute gains in earnings certainly does not explain fully the observed proportionally greater emigration of professionals. First, if more engineers and professionals do migrate than workers (proportionately to their total numbers), the differentials between nations should rapidly diminish, as was explained just above. Thus the flow should dry up quickly, leading to approximately equal net migration rates in each occupation. Second, the theory that most people have similar utility functions with declining marginal utility of income would suggest that the utility of a $3,000 gain to a worker may exceed the utility of a $9,000 gain to an engineer, so that in fact the former should be more willing to move than the latter.

The comparison of the utility of income between persons is a highly disreputable undertaking in specific cases. But a very few people would deny that the principle just expounded is valid. From this analysis it follows that the absolute income differences between laborers and engineers in two countries do not necessarily explain why highly trained people should feel more strongly motivated to emigrate than laborers.

Educational Attainment and Cosmopolitan Attitudes

However, there are several personal characteristics of the highly trained which tend to increase their mobility relative to that of the unskilled. The first of these tends to lower the psychic cost of migration. Scientists and engineers in practically all countries are required to study foreign languages, customs and cultures as part of their general training. This knowledge tends to make it easier to adjust to the environment of the country to which they migrate and may even make them derive positive utility from the adventures of travel and meeting the challenges of a new environment.

The broad and deep commitment to their profession characteristic of scientists and engineers manifests itself in the length of time they spend on their job *quasi*-voluntarily. On the average such people are much less dependent on social ties both in the old and new country of residence than are people keeping a strict seven-hour day, five-day work schedule. Moreover, the affinity of interests among professional colleagues and the relatively prestigious occupations of the migrants tend to create fairly ready and open social circles in the country of immigration.

Characteristics of Market Organization

Laborers and professionals have not only different personal characteristics which tend to make professionals comparatively more mobile, but they also sell their skills in separate markets. These markets have certain quality differences which increase the comparative mobility of professionals further.The world market for scientists and engineers is relatively small. As a consequence information about participants, their strengths and weaknesses, can be gathered quite cheaply and interpersonal comparisons over a wide segment of the market are feasible. The output of professionals, primarily their publications, are easily accessible and can serve as a basis for arriving at judgments about the quality of men. Personal contacts among professionals at international meetings furthermore facilitate the making of these types of judgments.

As a consequence many professional people migrate with employment contracts signed in their pockets, where the average unskilled worker has to rely on more-or-less imprecise information about entering the job market in the foreign country. The professional employment contracts often provide for payment of transportation costs by the employer, which at any rate are a much smaller proportion of a professional's annual earnings than they are of an unskilled worker's.

Difficulties of Changing Supply

Another force at work tending to increase the relative mobility of professionals has to do with the long time required to change effectively the rate of output and stock of professionals. While a suddenly increased demand for unskilled occupations is quickly filled because people can be trained in a short time, the situation is different for occupations that require many years of training, as most professional skills do. An increased demand for engineers and astronomers brought about by, for instance, a suddenly conceived national program for space exploration tends to raise the salaries of these professions far above equilibrium levels. Domestic supply will expand only slowly as an increased number of students are drawn into the study of physics and astronomy. In the meantime the excess demand spills over into countries where government policies have not disturbed the existing equilibrium of the labor market.

Sudden shifts in demand for professionals within countries develop not only in response to government policies but are also brought about by technical breakthroughs in industry and in the sciences. The development of computer technology, transistors, and jet engines has undoubtedly increased the demand for some special types of engineering and scientific skills, which the United States market was able to fill only slowly and which was in part met by the inflow of migrants. The excess demand for college teachers caused by the unusually large generation of students of college age is another case in point.

The sciences themselves go through cycles during which certain specialized areas attract temporary intensive attention, partly due to major discoveries, the availability of new research tools or perhaps even due to "fads." Often scientific research requires heavy investment in physical equipment and the economies from having many people use this equipment are substantial. These factors have led to the establishment of world centers for research in specialized areas and the productivity of scientists is increased manifold by their migration to these centers. None of these factors operate in the market for workers and the mobility of professionals is therefore likely to be higher than that of less-skilled people.

Just as supply of highly trained people responds only slowly to increased demand, so does supply respond with a lag when demand falls short of expectations. Decisions by government to open new universities, for instance, have to be made well in advance of the increase of demand for the skilled manpower. If the projected demand for the output of such a university falls short of expectations, then a temporary glut arises in the market, which may in part be relieved through emigration until either domestic demand catches up or supply gets reduced.

Apart from these surpluses and excesses, the movement of scientists, especially to the United States, can often be explained by the conditions of research available. This is particularly true of equipment. Many branches of physics, biology, and chemistry especially require very expensive research tools and laboratories. The United States, being a capital-rich country, is often able to provide scientists with this expensive equipment when their home countries cannot. It should be noted that the average capital endowment of American workers in all fields is higher than in any other country of the world, a phenomenon largely responsible for the higher income levels in the United States. The endowment of equipment for scientists in the United States, however, is likely to be much larger than this average and serves to add to the differential pull of scientists and workers.

Capital Gains from Foreign Training

It is worth emphasizing that the factors just presented have the effect of not only making scientists and engineers more likely than workers to emigrate from a given country, but also increasing their general mobility. The small, well-informed market, the low psychic cost of moving, the likelihood of persistent market disequilibria, the low cost of transportation relative to income all tend to make professionals everywhere respond quite readily to changed circumstances in the country of emigration, of destination or in third countries. Furthermore, a scientist visiting a foreign country increases his knowledge and experience, which in turn may raise his value to employers in his home country. The accompanying personal gains undoubtedly serve as motivation for many of foreign students and for other professionals accepting temporary professional positions abroad.

Weisbrod[6] has suggested that the gains from obtaining a high school degree are not limited only to the higher earnings a man can expect, but extend to his having the option to continue with higher education. This same kind of reasoning can be applied to a migrant. By taking a job abroad he opens to himself more options for future careers than he would have had available by staying at home. The range of alternatives thus opened is likely to be much greater for highly skilled individuals than for workers, so that this phenomenon tends to further increase the difference in the relative propensities to migrate of these two occupational groups.

Individual Attention by Governments

However, there are also certain potentially very important ways in which governments and industry can influence the mobility of highly trained personnel which are less effective in the case of unskilled workers.

Monetary rewards are only one, albeit a very important, dimension of most jobs. Other rewards, such as general status in society, involvement in affairs of state or of cultural importance, provide the individual with satisfaction and may have a value for him. Undoubtedly the power to influence people and to give orders attracts men to some jobs. Governments and industry have the opportunity to create positions with such characteristics specifically for deserving people with high skill levels, thus com-

[6]B. Weisbrod, *External Benefits of Public Education: An Economic Analysis* (Princeton: Princeton University Press, 1964).

pensating for the monetary advantages offered by employment in a foreign country.

Examples of such institutional arrangements are the creation of prestigious endowed chairs at universities, the creation of research institutes, the invitation to individuals to serve as directors in industry, advisors to government agencies, parliamentary committees and cultural activities. It is clear that the scope for such action by countries trying to keep prominent scientists, engineers and professionals from leaving is rather limited and may be met by countermoves in the countries trying to attract these men. But it appears to be true that these methods have in fact succeeded in some countries and have both prevented the departure and induced the return of some prominent scientists, engineers and professionals.

Chapter 3

THE THEORY OF MIGRATION AND HUMAN CAPITAL

Whenever a country loses a productive inhabitant through emigration the total value of the nation's output, its military and economic powers are reduced. Any person, therefore, who considers these magnitudes to be relevant targets of social and economic policies, judges the emigration of highly skilled and productive persons to be an unmitigated loss. Perhaps the recent concern over the brain drain is the manifestation of a widespread revival of nationalism, under which these policy targets have great prominence.

However, enlightened politicians throughout the world consider the maximization of the welfare of those at one time born within the country's territory to be the target to which the nation's energies and policies should be directed. The most important ingredient of welfare of concern to economists, is the level of income society has for distribution among its citizens. The theoretical analysis of the present chapter is directed at finding out what happens to aggregate and per capita incomes and the next chapter analyzes what happens to the welfare of the population of a country when highly skilled persons emigrate.

From the economist's point of view the distinguishing characteristic of human migration known as the brain drain is the large amount of human capital moving with the migrant. The present chapter attempts to integrate the theories of migration and human capital in a simple framework of comparative statics, thus focusing on the analysis of conditions in equilibrium before and after emigration of highly skilled persons.

EFFECTS ON AGGREGATE AND PER CAPITA OUTPUT

We assume the existence of a stationary economy with a constant labor force (L, equal to the population),[1] capital stock (K), technology, and tastes. Only one commodity (Y) is produced. All productive resources are perfectly divisible and owned collectively. There is an equal distribution of income, resulting initially in a per capita income

$$YC_o = \frac{Y_o}{L_o} \text{ per year.}$$

[1]The following analysis is facilitated by the assumption that all persons are members of the work force. Otherwise the expression for per capita income changes becomes unduly complicated and it would become necessary to trace the effects of an emigrating non-working member of the population. Such an analysis would add nothing to the main point of this chapter.

The aggregate production function consists of the components shown in Figure 3.1. In the southeast quadrant of this graph is found a map of isoquants representing the combinations of workers and physical capital capable of producing given quantities of the product Y per year. Although the production function is conveniently assumed to be linear-homogeneous, the specific shape of the isoquants is not important for the present purposes of analysis so long as it is true that movement along any ray from the origin leads to successively higher output.

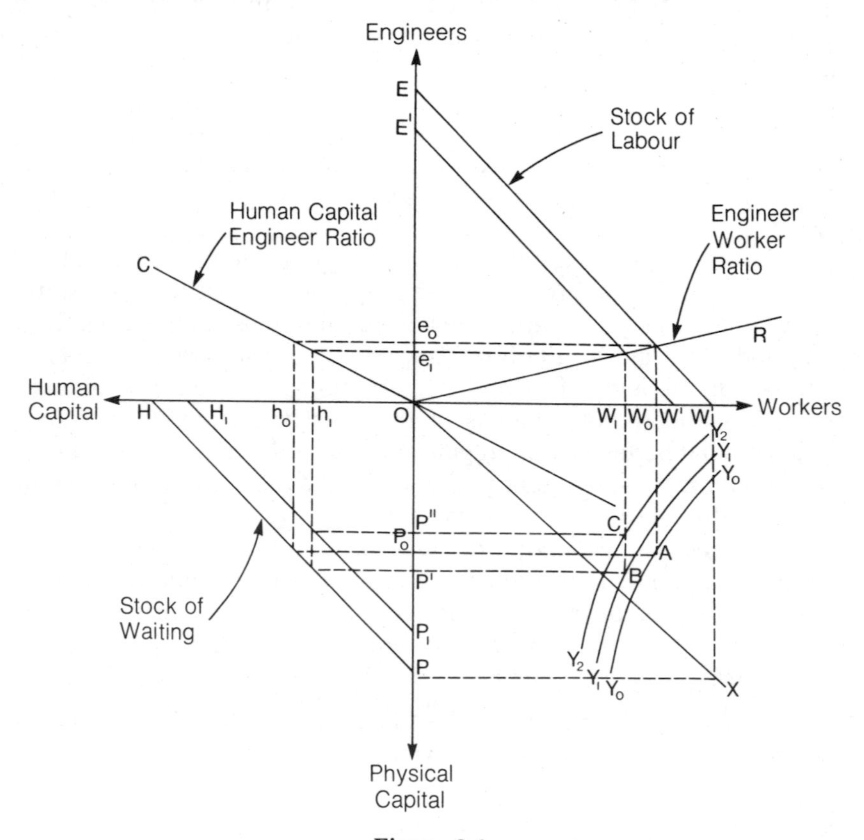

Figure 3.1

Output Effects in the Long-Run

The workers are "raw labor": unskilled and inexperienced. Human capital is *not* embodied in everyone. In this way, for a first step, we attempt to keep human capital as a separate factor of production.

The human capital element enters into the analysis in the remaining three sectors of the diagram. The first component of this element is the distinction between two skill groups of the labor force, workers and engineers. For heuristic purposes we assume at first that workers are completely unproductive unless they are supervised by a fixed number of engineers, as for example in the ratio of 100 workers per each engineer. Such a ratio is represented by the slope of the line OR in the northeast quadrant. Given the stock of labor in the economy there could be either OE engineers, OW workers or any other combination of the two skill-groups along the line EW. Given the assumption about the required combination of workers and engineers, the efficient numbers of workers and engineers are OW_0 and Oe_0 respectively.

The second component of the human capital element is found in the remaining two quadrants. In order to reflect the social option of using resources for the formation of either human or physical capital,[2] we assume that the country's capital stock consists of a given number of units of "waiting" which periodically, once a year, decomposes into a formless mass and can then costlessly be reallocated between human and physical capital. Workers are assumed to require zero human capital while it takes a certain number of human capital units to train a worker into an engineer. The specific human capital requirements of engineers is shown by the slope of the line OC in the northwest quadrant.

The total quantity of capital available in the economy can be used either all for human capital OH, all for physical capital OP, or a combination of uses shown by the line HP. Since Oe_0 engineers require Oh_0 human capital there is OP_0 capital left to equip the workers with machinery. Point A on isoquant Y_0 in the southeast quadrant thus represents the highest output the economy can produce with the available stock of labor, efficiently allocated between workers and engineers, and the available stock of capital, efficiently distributed between education and machines.

It must be emphasized that the assumption of a linear homogeneous production function between workers and physical capital is valid only when the engineers and human capital allocations are efficient in the sense just described. Because of the fixed and constant relationships between engineers and workers and physical and human capital, the production function is linear homogeneous also with respect to total labor force and total capital whenever the efficiency criteria are met.

This basic model can now be used to demonstrate the effects on national output and output per capita resulting from the emigration of an engineer and a worker. The following discussion distinguishes long-run and short-run effects.

The Long-Run

The long-run is characterized by the fact that after emigration, the remaining labor and capital may be reapportioned so as to assure maximum total

[2]This model of human-physical capital substitutability underlies the work of T. W. Schultz, "Reflections on Investment in Man," *Journal of Political Economy*, Supplement 70 (October 1962), and G. Becker, *Human Capital* (New York: National Bureau of Economic Research, Columbia University Press, 1964).

output with the new amount of resources. Thus, the effect of the emigration of a worker is merely that the stock of labor line in the northeast quadrant is shifted inward from EW to E′W′, while the capital stock line remains unchanged. Efficient combination of resources leads to output point B, which lies on isoquant Y_1, and which is found by reasoning identical to that used in finding point A.

The emigration of an engineer, however, causes not only the same inward shift of the labor line as does the emigration of a worker, but also causes the capital stock to fall by an amount equal to the units of capital required to train a worker into an engineer. Schematically, this reduction in society's capital stock is shown by the inward shift of the total capital line HP to H′P′. After emigration of the engineer, therefore, efficient allocation of the economy's resources leads to attainment of point C and isoquant Y_2 in the southeast quadrant.

It is now possible to compare the relative magnitudes of Y_0, Y_1, and Y_2 outputs which are attained originally, after emigration of a worker and of an engineer respectively. According to the diagram and the preceding reasoning point B must lie on a lower isoquant than point A. The economy has lost one unit of labor and, as long as labor has a positive marginal productivity, total output must fall. For analogous reasons point C must always be on a lower isoquant than A or B because the engineer's emigration caused a fall in available capital as well as labor, both of which initially had positive marginal productivity. This analysis thus shows that a nation's *aggregate output* will be reduced by any emigration, but it will be reduced more by the emigration of a highly skilled person.

Next, we turn to the analysis of the effects emigration has on *per capita output*. On the assumption of a linear homogeneous production function, the reduction of capital and labor inputs by an equal proportion lowers total output by the same proportion. Thus, there are three possibilities. First, at one extreme, an emigrating worker or engineer may take with him precisely his per capita share of the total social (human and physical) capital. Then labor, capital and output all fall by the same proportion. Output per head is unchanged.

Second, an emigrating worker takes no capital at all. His unequipped departure reduces slightly the number of engineers that must absorb capital and raises the amount of physical capital both absolutely and per worker. The fall in output is therefore smaller than in the first case, or than if an engineer leaves unequipped with physical capital. Average output rises.

Third, an engineer or worker may take capital, but either more-or-less than his per capita share of total social capital. The fall in total output will exceed that caused by a single unequipped worker's departure. The change in per capita output will be positive if the emigrant takes less than per capita capital and negative if he takes more.

In Figure 3.1, in which it is now assumed that no one migrates with physical capital, it can be easily seen whether an engineer's departure raises or lowers per capita income. The slope of the line OX (SE quadrant) indicates the average endowment of the total labor force (workers and engineers) with total capital (human and physical). Similarly the line OC has a slope equal to the average capital embodied in an engineer. If an engineer's embodied capital equals total capital per member of the labor force, the two slopes will be equal (that is, their slopes with respect to the capital axes OH and OP respectively). Whether they are equal can be tested by folding the four-quadrant diagram along a line running SE-NW at 45° through the origin. If OX folds up to OC, the ratios are equal. If OC lies south of OX, engineers are more capital-intensive than the whole work force, and an emigrating engineer causes per capita income to fall. If OC is north of OX, per capita income rises.

Unfortunately, actual per capita income may be changed by migration through other mechanisms than those described here. For example, if the capital-rich, high income people leave, per capita income will fall even if the rich and the poor had never worked together as in the model above (and even if the capital-rich had never rented their capital to the capital-poor as in Harry Johnson's Case 1).[3]

Per capita income may fall merely because it is averaged over a population with slightly fewer higher incomes.

The present model suggests the importance of the existing critical ratio of total social capital to manpower. It is interesting to examine the real world counterparts of these quantities. For the United States in 1957, T. W. Schultz has assembled estimates of the value of total human capital plus reproducible tangible wealth,[4] arriving at a figure of $2,465 billion. With an estimated population that year of 171 million, the average value of capital per person was $14.4 thousand. This compares with the human capital value of a person with two years of college education in 1957 of about $14.3 thousand.[5] On the basis of these admittedly rather rough estimates and the preceding analysis, U.S. per capita income would be raised in the long run by the emigration of any person with less than two years of college education and lowered if the emigrant had more than two years of college.

Unfortunately, similar estimates of capital values cannot be made readily for other countries, especially not for less developed nations. However, if roughly similar ratios were to be found, the emigration of moderately-educated persons, such as high school graduates with little college education (like those who came to the United States for further

[3]H. G. Johnson, "Notes on the Effects of Emigration of Professional People on the Welfare of Those Remaining Behind" (mimeo).

[4]Schultz, "Reflections on Investment in Man."

[5]See Chapter 10.

training), tends to *raise* per capita incomes in their native countries. If this speculation is correct then, given the restrictions most countries have imposed on general immigration but not on the immigration of highly skilled persons, sending students abroad to become permanent emigrants is an efficient method of raising per capita income.

Short-Run Effects

For the purpose of the present analysis the short-run is defined as that span of time during which it is impossible first, to reallocate units of waiting efficiently between human and physical capital or second, to redistribute physical capital efficiently to retain equal endowment per worker.

Starting with the same basic model as before, Figure 3.2 shows that upon emigration of a worker, W_0 to W_1, output falls from A (on Y_5) to B′ (on Y_3) if the original endowment of each worker with *physical* capital is retained, i.e., output takes place along the ray OY. On the other hand, the emigration of an engineer, shown as a move from e_0 to e_1, reduces the number of supervised and, therefore, productive workers from W_0 to W′ with an accompanying output loss of Y_5-Y_1, i.e., movement from A to A′.

The size of these short-run losses of output from emigration depends decisively on three factors. First, the length of time required to redistribute existing physical capital equally among the remaining workers. If technology is such that this process can occur only once a year when all capital decomposes, then the loss due to an emigrating worker is $(Y_5 - Y_3)$ T, where T is the fraction of the year between the date of emigration and the date of the annual capital reallocation. The loss due to the emigration of an engineer analogously is $(Y_5 - Y_1)$ T. However, if it is possible to redistribute physical capital immediately after emigration and at zero cost among the remaining workers, so that output takes place along AP_0 instead of OY, then the full use of the existing physical capital OP_0 assures that the emigration of a worker reduces losses to $(Y_5 - Y_4)$ T and of an engineer to $(Y_5 - Y_2)$ T. It is obvious that in between the two cases considered the losses are smaller the more readily physical capital can be reallocated the greater the cost of reshaping physical capital.

Second, the short-run losses depend on the duration of the disequilibrium situation. In the basic model it was assumed that the formation of human capital takes place only once-a-year upon decomposition of the entire capital stock. If engineers can emigrate on any date after the once-a-year reallocation, a steady flow implies that on the average an engineer cannot be replaced for one-half year. In the real world this half year has its equivalent in the training period of an engineer. This period is empirically observable and short-run output losses are smaller the shorter the training period.

Third, the short-run losses of output depend on the substitutability of engineers for workers. In the present model it is assumed that workers and

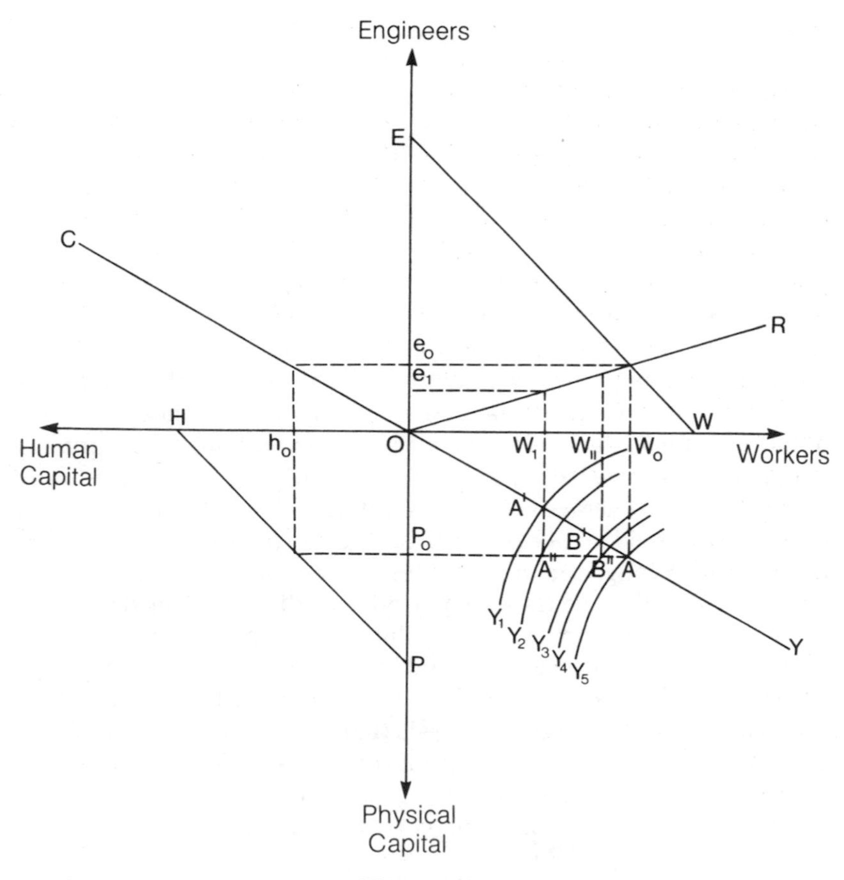

Figure 3.2

Short-Run Losses of Output

engineers are completely unproductive unless they are cooperating with each other in fixed proportions. This fact is responsible for the drastic fall in output following the emigration of one engineer, since it left W_oW' workers unemployed. In the real world it is likely that even without further training there is some substitutability between engineers and workers, most likely as a result of less supervision, i.e., the employment of fewer engineers per 100 workers. Unfortunately, the effect of such substitutions cannot be shown on the graph since logically it results in a different production function between workers (as supervised) and physical capital and thus would require redrawing of the entire isoquant map. In principle, however, short-run output losses are smaller the greater the substitutability of workers and engineers without added investment in training. The absolute gains from such substitutability are greater for an engineer's emigration than a worker's, and greater the larger the number of workers per engineer in the original technology. In the case of complete substitutability, the distinction between the two groups of labor disappears, and emigrations of workers and engineers result in equal losses.

In general the preceding analysis suggests that the emigration of an engineer leads to greater short-run losses than does the emigration of a worker but that this difference is decreased by the substitutability of workers for engineers, the malleability of physical capital and any decrease in the training period for engineers.

An empirical analysis of the immigration of scientists and engineers to the United States during the period 1957-66 has yielded the following results bearing on the present analysis.[6] Forming a ratio of the percentage of scientists and engineers in a country's total number of migrants to the United States and the percentage of scientists and engineers in the total population of the emigrant's native country, it was found that such highly skilled persons are ten times more likely to migrate to the United States than are persons of average skills. This indicates that short-run losses of the nature just discussed may be large if substitution possibilities are small and training periods long.[7] However, empirical estimates of the various substitution possibilities and training periods just discussed need to be undertaken before more detailed cost calculations can be made.

The importance of training period length leads on to the more dynamic problem of continuous loss of highly skilled persons from some countries. The simplified analysis above suggests that such countries should set their training rates high enough that emigration does not endanger the ratio of skilled to unskilled workers. Doing so will completely prevent short-run losses due, say, to a lack of improperly supervised workers, or a wrong ratio of engineers to physical capital.

In general, dynamic extensions of the preceding model can be undertaken at many different levels of complexity. They are of considerable interest in the analysis of growth models and have recently been undertaken.[8]

[6]See Chapter 7 for the source and derivation of the following statistics.

[7]Since these calculations have been made evidence has been produced that the U.S. data on the immigration of scientists and engineers represent a serious overstatement of the true flow. See Chapter 5.

[8]A. Berry and R. Soligo, "Some Welfare Aspects of International Migration," *Journal of Political Economy* 77 (September/October 1969).

Chapter 4

THE WELFARE APPROACH TO MIGRATION AND HUMAN CAPITAL

The analysis in the preceding chapter employed only technical relationships. In general, there was no mention of income redistribution effects as between different groups of individuals as owners of specific quantities of factors of production in the form of labor, human and real capital. Prices of these factors were completely left out of the analysis.

In order to deal with questions of welfare as contrasted with income alone, particularly the welfare gains and losses of different groups of owners of productive resources, we now turn to the analysis of a market economy where factor payments are determined by marginal productivity theory and the quantity of labor and human and real capital owned by each person. We commence the analysis by assuming perfectly functioning competitive markets and then in successive sections introduce more complex and realistic assumptions about non-marginal changes, the flow of externalities, the presence of government activities, and the financing of education.

MARGINAL MIGRATION—NO GOVERNMENT, NO EXTERNALITIES

Consider a world with no government, only privately financed education and no externalities either in production or consumption. In such a world the departure of a marginal quantity of a factor of production leaves unaffected the incomes of those remaining behind because, according to the marginal productivity theory of wages, the income of the factor of production is equal to the value of his contribution to output and the emigrating factor thus takes along both its contribution and claim to total output.

The marginal productivity theory of factor payments on which this important conclusion is based has a thorough foundation in economic theory. It follows from the assumption that employers are profit maximizing and tend to pay their workers in accordance with their contribution to the value of the firm's output. Thus, if an employee is very productive and underpaid, the market system assures that competitors will find out about this person and try to hire him or that he himself will be dissatisfied with his employment. The resultant offers from competitors and the entry into the labor market tend to raise his salary until it reflects more nearly the value of his contribution to output. Similarly, few firms can afford to pay employees wages exceeding the value of their contribution to the firm's output and stay in business. This process is judged to work quite well, on the average, even if there are exceptions of both under and overpaid persons at any given moment in time. High geographic and occupational mobility of labor are indications that this mechanism is at work continuously.

It is clear that under these assumptions the effects of emigration on the incomes of those remaining behind are nil and the same whether a highly skilled or unskilled person leaves. At the same time, however, the statistical average income of those remaining tends to fall when a skilled and rise when an unskilled person leaves simply because of the above and below average incomes of the migrants as discussed in the preceding chapter.

NON-MARGINAL CHANGES—NO GOVERNMENT, NO EXTERNALITIES

Let us now turn to the case where non-marginal quantities of productive factors leave a country. The resultant modifications of the analysis can best be brought out with the help of Figure 4.1, where the MPL_0 line shows the traditional marginal productivity of labor schedule as a decreasing function of the quantity of labor employed with a given stock of human and physical capital. At a stock of labor OL_0 the wage is OW_0. The emigration of L_1L_0 unskilled labor raises wages to OW_1 at the expense of resident capital owners. But the total income redistributed to the remaining labor, W_0ACW_1, is smaller than that lost by the resident owners of capital W_0BCW_1. The missing quantity is the "deadweight loss" of income represented by the area ABC. This reduction in the country's output is absorbed by the owners of capital and is in addition to the loss they experienced from the redistribution of W_0ACW_1 income to labor.[1] An analogous deadweight loss accrues to labor if a non-marginal quantity of capital is removed. This can be seen easily by considering a marginal productivity of capital schedule analogous to the marginal productivity of labor schedule in Figure 4.1 and by tracing through the strictly analogous consequences of a non-marginal loss of capital.

The income redistribution and output effects just discussed resulted from the assumed departure of only one factor of production in a two-factor world. However, as was argued above, the characteristic of highly skilled emigrants is that they take along a certain amount of capital and the basic model now has to be adjusted to account for the simultaneous loss of labor and capital.[2] A reduction in capital is represented by a downward shift of the MPL_0 curve to MPL_1 as shown in Figure 4.1. How great the shift is depends on the amount of capital departing.

If there are constant returns to scale, and if the original MFL curve is linear, we may deduce the characteristics of the shift. If the migration reduces both labor and capital by the same, say x per cent, then in the new

[1] This argument has been made first in the context of the brain drain problem by Berry and Soligo in "Some Welfare Aspects of International Migration."

[2] For a first exposition of this analysis see our "The International Flow of Human Capital: Reply," *American Economic Review* 58 (June 1968).

equilibrium output as represented by the area under the new MPL curve must have fallen by the same x per cent and the marginal product of labor must be unchanged. Figure 4.1 is constructed to satisfy these conditions. As migration reduces the labor force to L_1 the exodus of capital causes the MPL curve to shift in such a way that at the equilibrium point A the wage is reestablished at W_0.

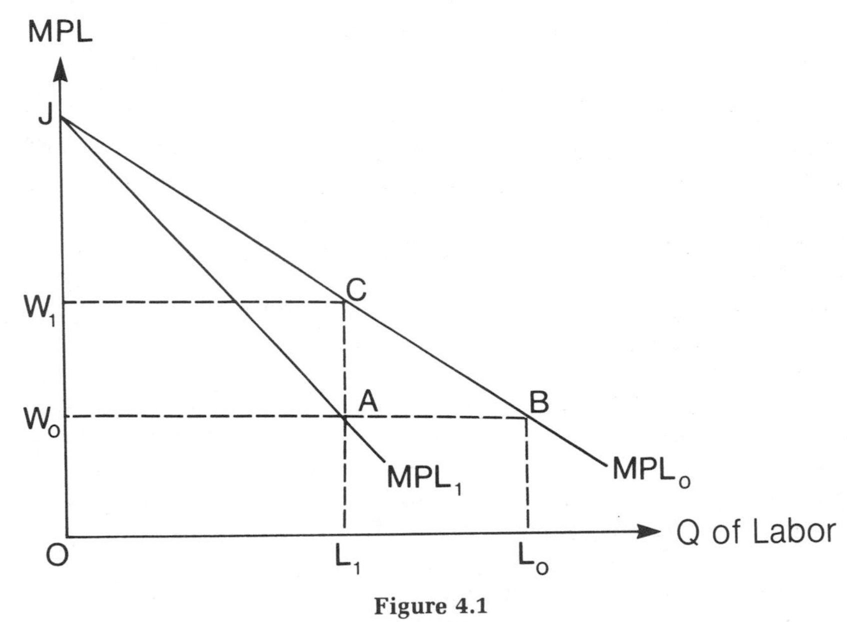

Figure 4.1

Deadweight Losses

The proof that total output under these assumptions falls also by x per cent proceeds by the comparison of the wage and capital shares in total output before and after the shift. The wage-rectangle originally OL_0BW_0 is reduced proportionately to the x per cent reduction in labor L_1L_0/OL_0 since only the base of the rectangle is changed by this amount and the height remains constant. The two rectangular areas JW_0B and JW_0A representing capital income shares before and after the change respectively have the same height but a base differing by x per cent. Thus the new capital income area must be x per cent less than the old. Therefore, the combined areas under the new MPL curve are x per cent smaller than under the original MPL curve.

We have thus shown that if the emigration of highly skilled persons removes equal proportions of labor and social capital, which implies that the emigrants' capital labor ratio is equal to society's overall capital labor ratio, then income and relative prices of remaining capital and labor are unchanged. More generally, income losses and redistribution effects from non-marginal losses of factors of production are an increasing function of the absolute difference between the ratios of capital to labor taken along by the emigrants and existing in the economy.

Economists are unable to assess quantitatively the overall welfare effects of such income redistributions and reductions in income experienced by the population remaining in the country. However, it is theoretically possible that in spite of the output losses a country's aggregate welfare rises. Such an event would occur when, as in Figure 4.1, L_0L_1 laborers emigrate and the increase in the welfare of the remaining labor brought about by the addition to their income of W_0ACW_1 exceed the loss of welfare of capital owners whose income is reduced by W_0BJ. Moreover, even if the aggregate welfare of this remaining population is reduced it is possible that the welfare gains of the emigrating labor itself more than compensate for these losses, so that the overall welfare of the country's former population is increased by the non-marginal emigration. We have argued above that government policies should rationally be concerned with the maximization of the welfare of this group of persons.

In the real world, of course, non-marginal emigration may increase or decrease welfare of those remaining behind and the total original population. The problem is that gains and losses cannot be established scientifically because interpersonal comparisons of utility cannot be made. This is why there is so much room for disagreement among well informed persons about the consequences of the brain drain. Perhaps it can be argued that the ultimate judgment over such welfare effects should be left to the parliaments of the affected countries in which democratic political processes produce policies tending to maximize the country's welfare, thus making indirectly the interpersonal comparisons of utility. The preceding analysis suggests that on *a priori* grounds the income redistribution and losses resulting from non-marginal migrations of highly skilled persons may either increase or decrease welfare.

The relevance of the preceding theoretical analysis to the problem of the brain drain in the real world depends decisively on whether recent migrations of highly skilled persons have been marginal or not. The empirical evidence presented in Part II of this book suggests that for most countries the net and even the gross losses of highly skilled persons represent relatively insignificant fractions of total manpower and of stocks of persons in specific skill groups.

MARGINAL CHANGES, GOVERNMENT AND NO EXTERNALITIES

Returning now to the analysis of welfare effects when the migration involves only marginal migrations of capital and labor, we consider what effect the emigrants' net fiscal contribution to government activities has on the welfare of those remaining behind when a highly skilled person emigrates.

Highly skilled persons tend to have above average incomes and pay above average taxes to their governments. Because of this fact it is often argued that the emigration of highly skilled persons reduces the welfare of those remaining behind since they have to tax themselves more heavily to retain the previous level of government revenue. This argument is misleading since it fails to take account of the fact that total government revenue is irrelevant for the welfare calculus. The emigrant takes along his contributions and a claim on government services and a welfare loss to those remaining behind occurs only to the extent that the emigrant's contributions to government resources exceed claims upon it.

Many government services, such as police and fire protection, judicial services, roads, etc., are normally demanded by persons in proportion to their incomes. Defence, on the other hand, is rather indivisible, and accrues to all citizens equally so that average tax rates may have to be raised when a person emigrates. The losses of those remaining behind are positive also in connection with government welfare programs designed to redistribute income from those with high to those with low incomes because the more educated emigrants tend to have above average incomes.The quantitative effect of the emigration of highly skilled persons on the tax rates necessary to maintain an equal level of defence and welfare services depends not only on the degree of progressiveness of the tax structure and the relative income of the emigrants, but also on their number. Historically, the numbers of these emigrants have been relatively small and therefore would have tended to affect the tax rates only very marginally.

One other significant government activity through which emigrants affect the welfare of those remaining behind is the provision of free public education. The magnitude of this welfare effect depends on the expectations of those involved in obtaining an education and those paying for it. One set of expectations is that, regardless of whether education is privately or publicly financed, families, directly, or as taxpayers in the currently productive generation, pay for the education of the young. If one holds these expectations, then the emigration of the young does not disappoint any expectation, nor reduce welfare. These emigrants only have an obligation to their children, who accompany them when they emigrate.

Under an alternative set of expectations children are raised and educated as an investment by family units to assure the parents' welfare on their retirement. Society as a whole taxes itself to gain the benefits associated with living in an educated population. According to this interpretation, educated emigrants owe a debt to the family unit if their education was privately financed and to society to the extent to which their educational expenditures were subsidized publicly. Then emigration (without remittances) does disappoint expectations and reduces welfare.[3]

[3]The first set of expectations corresponds to the "interdependent" utilities of 2a; the second set corresponds to their "independent" utilities, using the terminology developed by M. Blaug, "Optimal Wage and Education Policy with International Migration" (mimeo). For a

Which of these two sets of expectations is appropriate cannot be decided on *a priori* grounds. Perhaps families and societies are motivated both by a moral obligation and by the desire to make an investment in the externalities of education. However, the more weight is put on the moral obligation aspect, the less the welfare cost of the brain drain. In the absence of any precise measures of the various components of the brain drain falling upon those remaining behind, every observer has to make his own estimates. However, the earlier analysis has shown that such cost estimates are very sensitive to assumptions about the extent to which highly skilled persons pay for government services they don't consume, public goods are indivisible, government activities redistribute income, and parents "owe" an education to their children.

MARGINAL CHANGES, NO GOVERNMENT BUT EXTERNALITIES

Externalities is a term used by economists to refer to the effects a person's activities have on the well-being of others and for which he is neither compensated nor charged. It is argued that highly skilled people, especially scientists, produce many positive externalities for society so that their emigration tends to produce large uncompensated losses.

Before the importance of this proposition is analyzed in detail an important distinction between two types of externalities needs to be made. First, there is the externality associated with any practitioner of a profession or skill, such as that of a medical doctor. Losses from emigration of a doctor are limited to the period until a replacement has been trained and the flow of positive externalities reinstituted. Externalities in this sense give rise to short-run losses akin to and in addition to the short-run production losses analyzed earlier.

The second type of externality is associated with the emigrating person, apart from his skill. Thus, some persons have extraordinary qualities of leadership and productivity which are the result of particular intellectual gifts and personality make-ups and which are lost to society through the individual's departure. It is in connection with these kinds of externalities that the emigration of highly skilled persons leads not only to short-run but permanent, irreplaceable losses.

However, much care must be exercised in assessing this type of loss, especially when attributed to scientists producing knowledge of importance for the welfare of a society. Some common fallacies in the attribution of such losses are as follows.

First, knowledge is usually a free good. If an Indian scientist discovers the cure for cancer at Berkeley, his countrymen will benefit as much as if he had discovered it in Bombay. Second, as all teachers know, it is extremely

quite different approach, dealing with potential emigrants as choosers among different redistributive constitutions, see E. G. West, "Welfare Economics and Emigration Taxes," *Southern Economic Journal*, 36, 1 (July 1969): 52-57.

difficult to predict a student's success in professional life. Similarly, it is impossible to predict which scientist doing research in physics, chemistry, sociology or economics will make a key discovery. For this reason national science policy in most countries supports a number of research workers with more-or-less equal expectations of their success. The total outlay presumably reflecting a social investment appropriate for the expected result. Foreign employers similarly have no magic formula for picking men with expected especially high rates of return in their work. Third, for the reasons just presented and because scientists working in developed countries often have equipment and libraries not available to them at home, it is erroneous to reason that highly successful, emigrant scientists would have produced the same findings in their native countries. For every highly successful foreign-born and foreign-educated scientist in a given country there are a number of such foreign nationals producing average or below average output while being paid salaries reflecting more closely the average productivity of their scientific discipline. Fourth, the quality of "leadership" is difficult to define, and requires special conditions to develop and become effective. If there is a tendency for leaders to be produced by events, losses of potential leaders through emigration are much less serious than if the contrary is true. Fifth, while it is often argued that the brain drain is most serious when it takes applied, not basic, technical manpower, this point can easily be exaggerated. Applied research also tends to benefit countries other than the one in which it is first put to use. Reductions in the cost of production or new product developments are spread through the world by competition. Licensing fees in a competitive world are set at a level just marginally below the cost at which it pays to develop a substitute patent or process so that there is a tendency for the results of applied research to become available at a price approximating the marginal cost of this development. Countries should therefore be indifferent as between producing this applied research on their own or buying it abroad.

Sixth, on the issue of national prestige from scientific achievement, it is worth noting that the scientists' native countries are perfectly free to claim these men as native sons (as the Germans claim Einstein), which in no way reduces the host country's right to be proud of its new citizen (as the United States was of Einstein).

It should also be noted that some highly skilled emigrants might have had negative externalities associated with their activities had they stayed at home. In many countries there exists an unhappy and demoralized unemployed academic proletariat which may even become an irrational source of social unrest. Any reduction in this form of unemployment benefits society. From this point of view the brain drain serves as a valuable safety valve for the release of pressures created by faulty manpower planning and the overproduction of highly skilled persons.

Other beneficial externalities accrue to society from the emigration of eminent scientists when their departure opens up opportunities for abler younger persons to move into positions of responsibility and influence. Also, the emigration may result in stirring up public concern and in a reexamination of existing institutions and practices whose unsuitability to modern conditions often is the cause of the emigration. Eminent persons abroad often continue to retain interests in the affairs of their native countries. Thus they can influence favorably policies made in their country of new residence and give counsel from a position of independence to governments and other institutions in their native country.

SUMMARY OF ARGUMENTS ON THE WELFARE EFFECTS OF MIGRATION OF THE HIGHLY SKILLED

In Chapter 3 we discussed the "nationalistic" preoccupation with the maximization of total output of a country. We showed that under such a preoccupation all emigration is undesirable since it reduces total output. The emigration of highly skilled and productive persons is particularly undesirable since it leads to relatively larger output losses than if unskilled persons emigrate. We then argued that the proper preoccupation of national leaders and therefore the proper focus of analysis is with the emigration induced changes in income and welfare of all the people living originally under their jurisdiction. Since most voluntary emigrants can be assumed to increase their welfare, the focus of the analysis is thus shifted to the effects emigration has on the income and welfare of those remaining behind.

In Chapter 3 we concentrated the analysis of the effects of migration on technical engineering relationships, thus abstracting from all problems caused by changes in income distribution by different groups of owners of productive resources in the economy. We showed that in the long run the amount of income available for distribution after emigration results in increased or decreased per capita income of the remaining population depending on whether the emigrants take along less or more than an "average" share of society's capital, respectively. We also identified the nature and causes of short-run adjustment costs which are superimposed on the long-run output effects and which may be particularly important in some of the developing countries.

The entire analysis of Chapter 3 is applicable to outflows of one or many persons with any level of skills. External and fiscal effects were not discussed. Conceptually these may be considered as having been reflected in the value of the economy's output of the one good. Alternatively, the present chapter's discussion of external and fiscal effects could be incorporated into the analysis by adjusting estimated income changes in terms of the real good for external and fiscal effects to arrive at the estimates of net welfare changes.

In the present chapter we assumed the existence of a market economy with given ownership of the factors of production and relative factor prices competitively determined. We then considered welfare changes induced by emigration on those remaining behind under various assumptions about the nature and effects of externalities and government activities.

We showed that marginal migration in the absence of externalities and government leaves unchanged income and welfare of those remaining behind. Non-marginal migration, on the other hand, reduces total output and may result in a redistribution of income. The owners of the factor of production made relatively more abundant by the emigration find the relative factor price turned against them. Their incomes are reduced by an amount redistributed to the relatively scarcer factor and by the amount of deadweight loss identified in the analysis. These income redistribution and reduction effects may increase or decrease overall welfare, depending on the marginal utilities of income of the gainers and losers. The welfare calculus may be expanded to include the welfare changes of the emigrants along with those remaining behind.

The last part of the present chapter considered the influence government activities and externalities have on the welfare of the remaining population when a marginal number of skilled persons emigrate. The welfare effects of these influences were seen to be complex and impossible to quantify. We attempted to speculate about the likely direction and magnitude of their influence. Thus we have identified and analytically isolated the effects of migration on income per capita in a statistical sense, on the income of individual groups of owners of productive resouces, on welfare through income redistribution, short-run adjustment, externalities and fiscal effects. Clearly, this classification scheme was adopted only for analytical and expositional convenience. In the real world, all of these effects are likely to overlap and occur in combinations.

Part II

EMPIRICAL STUDIES

Chapter 5

PRACTICAL AND CONCEPTUAL PROBLEMS OF MEASURING THE BRAIN DRAIN

In Chapters 3 and 4 of this book we have argued that policy makers should be concerned with the effects the migration of highly skilled persons has on the welfare of the people remaining behind. We showed that in a market economy without government and externalities marginal changes leave incomes of the non-emigrating population unchanged and that the crucial magnitudes to be considered in any policy decisions therefore are the income redistribution effects associated with government activities, the externalities and the short-run adjustment costs existing in the real world. For non-marginal changes, in addition, the deadweight losses or gains are of some importance. It would therefore seem to follow that the empirical part of this book would be concerned with measuring the influence on welfare resulting from the brain drain and operating through government activities, externalities, adjustment costs and the losses of surplus. However, we were unable to make such estimates, for the simple reason that the necessary raw data are not available.

This is unfortunate, but the very nature of the government effects and externalities makes it highly unlikely that reliable estimates of the appropriate kind could ever be made. Not only are externalities and the benefits from government expenditures extremely pervasive, but they are built into certain prices and values as rents or quasi-rents. Beneficiaries have strong incentives to hide the true magnitude of their gains because if they did reveal them they would face the risk of having to pay for them, or be taxed on them.

Like so many other social and physical scientists we found ourselves unable to measure what the theory tells us is important and had to turn to measuring magnitudes for which raw data and techniques *are* available, even if their relevance to the policy issues at hand is less direct and more tenuous. Thus, we had to confine the measurement of national "gains" and "losses" from the migration of highly skilled persons to the estimation of the numbers of migrants, current and past, and the value of the human capital embodied in this migration and in the international exchange of students. In our view, however, such calculations are important and useful for the following four reasons.

First, the statistics give precision to magnitudes which are discussed at great length by the public and which are considered to be relevant for policy making by persons who either do not know or do not understand the theoretical discussions of Part I, or who have explicitly rejected it as irrelevant or erroneous. Therefore, the empirical studies of this book will at least produce some reliable data and some idea of their limitations on the basis of which the magnitude of what many persons *believe* to be "gains" or "losses" from the brain drain from nation states can be used for policy discussions.

Second, countries which have a guilt conscience about the numbers of trained men they are receiving as "gifts" or as "loot" from poorer countries may be better able to persuade themselves to aid the sending nations if they know the value of the human capital in the brain drain. This statement is hardly open to argument—it is merely a hypothesis about what voters and statesmen find persuasive or compelling. Thus, we along with others have been publicizing the value of human capital embodied in foreign students who decide not to return home (see Chapter 10). It has been found that such estimates help to bring the "loss" of the sending countries into some kind of perspective, although this perspective must surely be of only marginal influence on policy formation regarding the much broader issue of student exchange and foreign development assistance.

Third, countries which receive highly qualified emigrants from other countries may be inclined to enter into negotiations to compensate the senders for their "gift" or "loss." The bargainers will require some standard estimates which can be easily understood and verified and the cost-of-human-capital figures meet these requirements. Thus, the sending country might argue that the capital embodied in the migrants is an estimate of the amount of capital which might have been used for other purposes and therefore is at least a rough indicator of the present value of future incomes it lost (forgetting that most of it would have been consumed by the emigrant and his offspring). Or they might take a more grimly commercial view and offer to "export" brains and skills at average cost. Finally, on some theoretical model or other of economic growth, or of economics of scale, they might argue that the absence of the embodied capital has delayed or prevented the growth of the incomes of the remaining population by a certain fraction of the estimate of the "gift."

Fourth, the measures represent an historical record of the magnitudes of labor and human capital flows in recent years. As such they are part of the growing body of verifiable, classified and somewhat digested knowledge which will be the raw material of research by future scholars whose purposes cannot be known at present.

Thus, while the empirical studies fall short of the ideal of testing theoretical propositions developed by *a priori* reasoning or of providing inputs into cost-benefit calculations for policy makers directly, they nevertheless are of value and worth presenting. The fact that they already have been and undoubtedly will be, used by proponents of the nationalistic view of the problems raised by the brain drain to bolster their case is unfortunate, but is not sufficient reason for us to desist from publishing our estimates. Such wrong use is analogous to the use made of trade figures by those favoring a tariff on a certain product: detecting that its net trade flow is "unfavorable," they wrongly claim that a *prima facie* case has been made for protective duties. In trade, favorable balances in bilateral exchanges cannot be expected for more than about half of a country's trade relations; otherwise, imports would not be received for exports. The net balance is simply uninformative, for policy purposes. Likewise, a net balance on human-capital flows with any other country, or with all other countries taken together, is uninformative. Unless seen in the context of all a country's alternative education, manpower, migration, income redistribution and savings policies, and in the light of all its alternative links and flows to other nations, the size of a net or gross flow means nothing.

We profoundly hope that readers will attempt to understand the welfare arguments in Part I before making use of the empirical measures herein. These measures are not in themselves an adequate support for any particular change in policy, in that they do not indicate the impact of migration of educated persons on the welfare of remaining populations.

The remainder of this chapter is devoted to the discussion of data sources for and the methodology of estimating first, the number of brain drain migrants and second, the human capital value brought along by the migrants or acquired by foreign students.

PROBLEMS OF DEFINING AND COUNTING BRAIN DRAIN MIGRANTS

Brain drain migrants have to be distinguished from temporary visitors such as students, trainees and technical experts on the one hand and permanent immigrants in general on the other. It is easy enough to *define*, from these points of view, the characteristics of a brain drain migrant: "A person is a brain drain migrant if he has the intention of holding permanent employment in a country other than the one in which he was educated up to a specified, high level."

The Organization for Economic Cooperation and Development, for purposes of a special study, has arbitrarily defined the population of the brain drain to be such persons as have undertaken higher education and obtained a university degree.[1] Eventually, perhaps, it will be possible to quantify the brain drain more accurately by assigning relative weights to various levels of educational attainment, such as 1.0 for a first university degree (e.g., the bachelor's degree in the United States), 1.5 for the Ph.D., .5 for completed high school, etc. Such a procedure avoids some of the arbitrariness of a single criterion but introduces its own problems of finding meaningful weights. In general the question of defining a migrant as a

[1] Organization for Economic Cooperation and Development, Committee for Scientific and Technical Personnel, *International Movement of Scientific and Technical Personnel* (Paris, 1965), mimeo.

brain drain loss is not independent of one's conception of the nature of the loss incurred through the migration.

Practical application of the preceding definition of a brain drain migrant by education attained runs into serious difficulties when it is attempted to formulate the criterion of "intention to hold permanent employment" in operational terms. Few migrants know whether they intend to stay permanently in a given country. Their intentions are constantly revised as opportunities for employment develop at home and in the country of new residence. Assuming for a moment that at the time of crossing borders it is possible in principle to distinguish those who intend to stay and those who do not, how could statisticians go about making the distinction? They could distinguish by types of visas issued, which presumably reflect intent. But there are important laws in most countries which make it advantageous to hide one's intentions. In the United States it paid to enter as a draft-exempt temporary student if one's age was less than 26. Persons older than 26 were free from military service obligations and had greater employment freedom if they entered as permanent immigrants even though they intended to stay only as trainees. For such reasons, the distinction of migrants by type of visa issued is unreliable.

Criteria based on length of actual stay are ambiguous because in many highly skilled professions it is impossible to say when an individual who came as a student or trainee starts to "work" and stops "learning." In the United States the recipient of a Ph.D. in many disciplines has ahead of him an important period of apprenticeship in teaching and research as an "assistant," albeit well-paid, professor before he is a genuinely qualified professional in his field.

Even the concept of "employment in another country" is ambiguous because of the existence of international organizations. Consider an international agency providing technical aid to less developed countries. It employs specialists from many countries, which through their contributions to the agency are indirectly the employers of these persons. Assignment of personnel of such agencies in particular countries is guided by special needs, recruitment by the availability of men with special skills, so that countries will typically not receive aid through the kind of specialists they have contributed to the pool and their own nationals will be employed in other countries. Some countries have deplored the hiring of their nationals by international agencies as an undesirable brain drain in spite of the fact that they are receiving an equivalent value of services for the ones their nationals provide to other countries.

However, these kinds of conceptual problems are common to all measurement in the social sciences and in practice they are solved by the adoption of "reasonable" conventions and more-or-less arbitrary definitions. Measurement of the brain drain phenomenon has run into added problems arising from the fact that researchers have to make do with raw data compiled for other purposes so that much of the information contained in them is useless in the application of reasonable conventions and definitions.

Thus, the most widely used statistics on recent brain drain flows have been compiled by the U.S. Immigration and Naturalization Service for the purposes of analysis and records relevant for the legal role and responsibilities of the U.S. Department of Justice. They are deficient and potentially misleading for the analysis of the brain drain because in the first place they fail to ascertain the highly skilled immigrants' true level of professional qualification. That is, standards of qualification for "biologists," "chemists," "economists," etc., vary widely. Furthermore, while there is an incentive for misreporting, no reliable method for ascertaining the accuracy of information is available. Second, the data do not permit distinction between highly skilled immigrants educated in the United States or elsewhere; that is, it matters whether a scientist whose "last residence" was Argentina received all or part of his education from Argentina, the United States or third countries. Lastly, the flow data do not account for homeward migration from the United States by scientists and scholars who earlier entered the United States with immigrant visas unimpeded by working restrictions imposed on holders of visitors' visas, even though they might always firmly have intended to stay only for temporary training and work experience.

How misleading the flow statistics of the U.S. Immigration and Naturalization Service can be has recently been shown by a careful case study. According to the official U.S. statistics Sweden was shown to have lost 106 scientists, engineers and doctors during the period 1957-61. A careful Swedish analysis of the educational qualifications of the emigrants at time of original entry to the United States, employing the OECD definition of brain drain emigrants, and measurement of the number of such emigrants who had returned to Sweden from the United States over the same period has shown that Sweden's loss was not 106 but only 25.[2] The number 25 may represent a serious loss but, if it does, the number 106 must be catastrophic in comparison.

In Chapter 7 we have nevertheless used the unadjusted data supplied by the U.S. Immigration and Naturalization Service, showing what kinds of analytical insights can be derived from flow data of the numbers of brainy migrants. Many of the calculations presented in that Chapter involve intercountry comparisons and ratios. The validity of rankings based on these ratios is unaffected by the shortcomings of the data just presented only to the extent that they are applicable with equal strength to all countries.

A second set of empirical studies presented in Chapters 8 and 9 are based on a set of raw data containing more of the basic information required

[2]G. Friborg, "Report of the Committee for Scientific and Technical Personnel, International Movement of Scientific and Technical Personnel" (Paris, OECD, August 1965) mimeo.

to measure the brain drain with the help of reasonable conventions and definitions. The set of raw data is the National Register of Scientific and Technical Personnel, which is maintained as a cooperative undertaking of the National Science Foundation and the scientific community, as represented by the scientific professional societies. Within this framework the Foundation develops uniform standards and procedures, and the cooperating professional societies undertake to identify and locate qualified scientists to insure the most complete coverage possible of those eligible for inclusion in the National Register if they have "full professional standing," as determined by the appropriate scientific society, whether or not they are members of a professional society.

The eligibility criteria vary among the societies, and in some fields the scope for inclusion is broad. For example, the American Chemical Society considers a person with a bachelor's degree in chemistry, and employed in a position requiring a knowledge of chemistry, a qualified chemist. In the field of experimental biology, on the other hand, the Federation of American Societies for Experimental Biology considers as fully qualified only those who hold the doctorate and have several years of research experience.

In an attempt to obtain complete coverage of the scientific community all known qualified scientists were requested to respond to the National Register questionnaire. Also included in the mailing lists are potentially qualified persons, such as recent graduates with science baccalaureate degrees, subscribers to professional publications, and non-member registrants at professional meetings.

In 1966, society mailing lists included 482,000 names of professional society members and others identified as having a technical interest in one of the natural or selected social science fields within the scope of the National Register. Duplicate names identified subsequently reduced this list to approximately 453,000 individuals. Of this number, 302,000 returned questionnaires, and 151,000 were non-respondents.Those providing incomplete information or not meeting registration criteria totaled 59,000; thus, 243,000 persons represented in the 1966 data were used in this study. In proportionate terms, 67 per cent of the individuals on the lists compiled by the cooperating societies returned questionnaires, and 20 per cent of the returned questionnaires were incomplete or lacking in full professional qualifications.

To determine the characteristics of the non-respondents, a sample based on geography and discipline has been developed and plans are underway to conduct a field study. Until this study has been completed, the degree to which the respondents are representative of the entire scientific community is uncertain.

The coverage of National Register has been continually improving, and it is estimated that the 1966 registration included most of the nation's science doctorates. Although the proportion varies in different scientific areas, it is believed that a substantial majority of those qualified for inclusion are in the National Register.

At present there is no information available as to whether foreign-born or foreign-educated scientists have a different propensity to return the questionnaire.

PROBLEMS OF HUMAN CAPITAL MEASUREMENT

In this book much use is made of the concept of human capital. By analogy with capital theory, this approach regards each person as having attached to him an amount of wealth equal to the present value of his net future earnings. While he cannot usually sell this wealth, as he would sell a machine or farm that he owned, he can increase its future earning power by investment in his schooling, on-the-job training, and occupational and regional mobility.

The importance of the approach is as the source of hypotheses about many kinds of behavior: people's investment in themselves should be in forms, amounts and periods which will both augment and maximize the value of their human capital, after making allowance for non-pecuniary types of income and for leisure. This application is clearly positive. It should lead to the prediction of decisions about schooling, location and jobs, and in aggregate, can help to explain group behavior or attitudes to investment in educational facilities, migration and collective bargaining concerning working conditions, pensions and retirement provisions.

At the same time, the human-capital approach has been used in a quasi-normative style in determining rates of return to buttress claims that too little (or too much) is being spent in aggregate on certain types of educational facilities, as opposed to social spending on physical capital and other forms of public goods.

In migration studies, both these approaches are present, and they ought to be clearly distinguished. Among the positive studies, Sjaastad,[3] Myers[4] and a number of other writers have explained how migration is to be regarded as investment in human capital, and have attempted some measurement of its pay-off or rate of return. The estimation of personal rates of return is difficult, chiefly because it is difficult to discover what migrants expect certain values to be. The aggregate rate of return, however, is just as difficult to estimate as an aggregate rate of return to schooling, because of the impossibility, short of a complete (planning) model, of knowing what rates of pay would exist if all categories of educated persons were to be changed. In migration studies, it is comparatively easy to learn or guess what personal incomes are believed to be in a certain region, but it

[3]L. Sjaastad, "Costs and Returns of Human Migration."

[4]R. G. Meyers, "Study Abroad and the Migration of Human Resources" (Ph.D. thesis, University of Chicago, 1967).

is impossible to guess what the pay levels would in fact become if everyone moved where his human wealth would be maximized.

Normative studies of migration not only suffer from the same difficulties (of data, and of aggregation) as the positive or behavioristic studies, but also from a perceptible tentativeness in the relevant welfare theory. As with similar problems in land and real estate appraising and valuation theory and practice, the measurement of the quantity of human capital migrating must, in a world of adjustment to disequilibrium in goods and factor markets, depend upon the purpose for which the measurement is to be used. Here are a few examples:

(1) the value of exports of human capital, analogous to the balance of trade or similar values of exports of machines and other capital goods;
(2) the "debt" of a migrant to his homeland;
(3) the "balance of indebtedness" between two countries exchanging migrants;
(4) the "supply price" of a country training additional emigrants for "sale";
(5) the "demand price" of a country importing additional emigrants instead of training its own people.

In the absence of human capital markets and during disequilibrium in labor markets, the values of these concepts will differ, though impatient economists may reason that in the long-run with perfect markets the differences would disappear.

Closer examination of the differences reveals that their source is in different assumed conditions in which some hypothetical transaction is to take place. We must ask what a certain price would be "if. . . ." For example, if there were a *stock* of nuclear scientists for sale, what short-run price would emerge from competition among the nations? Now, if nuclear scientists were produced for sale, what long-run price would be determined by interaction of both supply and demand? Third, if potential emigrants were to buy their right to leave from their remaining countrymen, how much would they offer? And how much would their countrymen demand?

As will be discussed later, a number of such questions can be posed and indeed have been suggested as bases for international compensation in brain drain exchanges and as variables in explaining total community outlays on education.[5] When the problem of finding quantitative answers is faced, however, only four actual techniques have been suggested:

(a) Cost-saving to the country of destination for the human capital received;
(b) Present value of the human capital migrating;
(c) The deadweight, or consumers'-surplus loss from migration;
(d) The reduction in the flow of savings taxes and public spending.

[5]Weisbrod, *External Benefits of Public Education*.

These techniques will be reviewed in the following section, emphasis being given to "cost-saving" estimates.[6]

(a) Cost-saving measures. This approach can best be summarized by suggesting the question which it directly answers: If an immigrant brings a certain education and experience with him, what are the direct resource costs and/or foregone earnings which are avoided by his new country? The answer, obviously, requires discovering that country's costs of schooling at various levels (average or marginal costs depending on whether he is part of a stream, or a single migrant); his foregone earnings (on the assumption that he might otherwise have migrated before his period of schooling and worked in his new country); or his maintenance costs (on the assumption that his new country might have sent someone to which he worked part-time).

In fact, such estimates follow very closely the methods pioneered by T. W. Schultz in estimating the human capital embodied in the U.S. labor force.[7] Difficult questions arise about whether or not to use domestic or foreign values, but most of the complexities of the method lie in problems of data. It has been extensively used by Grubel and Scott, Parai,[8] Wilkinson,[9] and in the present book.

(b) Present value of human capital migrating. The techniques of estimating the present value of the human capital embodied in migrants working from expected future earnings are already well examined in the M. J. Bowman and R. G. Myers article cited above,[10] and are best known in their employment by Weisbrod in his attempt to measure the gain and loss of human capital in Clayton County.[11] More recently, Rashi Fein has made a similar calculation for the American South,[12] and Myers himself has made interesting applications of the technique to the decisions of Peruvian students in the United States about where to live permanently.[13]

As with the cost-saving approach, it is necessary to know the numbers of persons migrating and their schooling. Their age becomes particularly

[6]For a review of (a) and (b) see M. J. Bowman and R. S. Myers, "Schooling, Experience and Gains and Losses in Human Capital Through Migration," *Journal of the American Statistical Association* 62 (September 1967).

[7]See especially T. W. Schultz, "Capital Formation by Education," *Journal of Political Economy* 68 (December 1960); and *The Economic Value of Education* (New York: Columbia University Press, 1963).

[8]L. Parai, *Immigration and Emigration of Professional and Skilled Manpower during the Postwar Period*, Special Study No. 1, Economic Council of Canada (Ottawa: Queen's Printer, 1965).

[9]B. Wilkinson, *Studies on the Economics of Education*, Occasional Paper No. 4, Economics and Research Branch, Department of Labor (Ottawa, 1965).

[10]Bowman and Myers, "Schooling, Experience and Gains and Losses. . . ."

[11]Weisbrod, *External Benefits of Public Education*.

[12]R. Fein, "Education Patterns in Southern Migration," *Southern Economic Journal* 32 (1965-66).

[13]Myers, "Study Abroad and the Migration of Human Resources."

important, as the method attempts to measure the value of income in the remaining working years. Obviously one of the most important questions for any particular study is the decision whether to use expected future incomes in the country of destination or the country of origin. If the aim is to estimate the incentive to migrate, present values in both places may be used, and increasing degrees of disaggregation (by age, sex and profession) will then be found to increase the understanding of migratory behavior.

However, the "normative" or policy usefulness of present value estimates of migrating human capital is not clear. Rashi Fein, indeed, draws no conclusions from his briefly reported valuation of southern migrations.[14] Bowman and Myers appear to place most stress on the capacity of the technique to weight accurately the differing age and skill compositions of a region's inflows and outflows, thus measuring migration's contribution (in comparison to schooling) to the formation of capital. This role can be approximated by cost-saving measures; Wilkinson and Parai, for example, both make much of the fact that Canada's net gain from immigration is not merely in differences in the numbers of "skilled" or "professional" people coming and leaving, but in the fact that the immigrants on the average embody more schooling than the emigrants.[15] Bowman and Myers,[16] and Fein, therefore, can be regarded as taking this examination one step further by turning from relatively insensitive costs-of-years-of-schooling estimates to more finely detailed expected earnings of various skills and professions. Their approach, therefore, is able to test the "paradox" that an equal exchange of equally schooled persons could raise the value of the stock of human capital in *both* regions; the years-of-schooling approach could not do this. But we are not convinced that this paradox is the kind of proposition that needs rigorous confirmation, except as propaganda to convince non-economists that specialization, the division of labor and mobility can be beneficial generally, not simply to the "net gainer" of educated persons.

(c) The dead-weight, or consumers'-surplus loss from migration. This approach, not strictly in the human capital stream of migration studies, is more in the tradition of the cost-of-monopoly and cost-of-tariff studies associated with A. C. Harberger and H. G. Johnson.[17] It does not place a value on the gross amount of human capital migrating, but only on the "loss of welfare" from a non-marginal emigration.

The concept itself has been discussed by Berry and Soligo,[18] H. G.

[14] Fein, "Education Patterns in Southern Migration"; also see the reference to his measurements in Bowman and Myers, "Schooling, Experience and Gains and Losses," p. 879.

[15] Wilkinson, *Studies on the Economics of Education*, p. 69.

[16] Parai, *Immigration and Emigration of Professionals*, p. 82.

[17] A. C. Harberger, "Using the Resources at Hand More Effectively," *American Economic Review* 49 (May 1954): 134-146; and Harry G. Johnson, "The Economic Theory of Customs Union," *Pakistan Economic Journal* 10 (March 1960): 14-32.

[18] Berry and Soligo, "Some Welfare Aspects of International Migration."

Johnson[19] and Chapter 4 above. Only Mishan has attempted to measure it, for the United Kingdom, assuming unitary elasticity of derived demand.[20]

(d) The loss of the flow of savings and of taxes. For completeness it is necessary to report on two proposed measures of national loss from emigration, capable of rough measurement. The first of these is the loss of future savings, investment or capital, and the second is the loss of transfers of public goods and expenditures from scientists to other citizens.

Future savings and growth: Consider a growing economy depending on savings and capital inflows for future per capita income growth. Such an economy may well attach more importance to the size and timing of these flows than to the dead-weight loss of current output. The brain drain will be seen as an outflow of capital which may be regarded as a "regrettable necessity," either unpreventable or desirable for reasons irrelevant here. The drain, however, is capable of producing future capital benefits via emigrant remittances homeward. The statistical problem of the "cost" of the drain, therefore, is to estimate the difference between the flow of savings, if the emigrants had remained at home (their income minus their consumption and transfers), and the flow via remittances (the recipients' income minus their consumption and transfers). This has actually been attempted in a study.[21] The underlying theory is also discussed by Charles Kindleberger.[22]

Indeed, a large number of growth models are, to the extent they are quantifiable, capable of measuring absolutely or comparatively the impact on the growth path and the equilibrium growth rate of an outflow of human capital.

Second, and finally, it would seem possible to undertake a study of the tax-and-transfer consequences of the brain drain for non-migrants. Harry Johnson, in an attempt to discourage the use of the present value of future incomes as a measure of national loss, has been particularly emphatic in stressing this valid alternative.[23] What is required is a benefit-cost, or with-and-without-migration analysis of the tax and transfer mechanism within the economy. In static terms, the emigrant will pay certain taxes from his expected income and receive certain specific benefits (i.e., with positive marginal cost). The difference between these two expected flows

[19]Johnson, "Some Economic Aspects of the Brain Drain," *Pakistan Development Review* 7 (Autumn, 1967): 379-411.

[20]E. J. Mishan, "The Brain Drain: Why Worry So Much?" *New Society* 10 (November 1967): 619-622.

[21]C. Michalopoulos, "Labor Migration and Optimum Populations," *Kyklos* 21 (1968).

[22]Charles Kindleberger, "Emigration and Economic Growth," *Banca Nazionale del Lavoro Quarterly Review* 18 (September 1965).

[23]Harry G. Johnson, in Walter Adams, ed., *The Brain Drain*, pp. 83-84, and his earlier contributions in *Minerva*. Johnson has, of course, also considered the general sources of loss: externalities and changes in factor proportions; see the appendix to his article in the *Pakistan Development Review*.

is a measure of the loss or gain of the non-migrating population. It is possible to make specific assumptions about whose taxes will increase and what benefits will be altered in the economy's post-migration adjustment; these will enable the benefit-cost analysis to determine which identifiable income groups, among the surviving population, will actually gain or lose.

In less static terms, the economist may be able to concentrate his attention on the impact of the migration on certain generations. To do so, however, requires that he make assumptions about the adjustment in the tax-and-transfer mechanism to reduce or maintain the net payments to older people (and *their* adjustments in retiring later and working harder); and to reduce or maintain the flows of payments for the welfare and education of younger generations. It is difficult to know how to make such assumptions satisfactorily, yet in the absence of the correct assumption, it is all too easy to bias such analyses to show that the "burden" is borne entirely by any of the three generations; old people, contemporaries, or children.

So far, only two clear facts are known: that brain drain migrants earn more than average taxpayers, and so presumably make a net fiscal contribution when they reside in an economy with a progressive fiscal system; and that their removal carries both a tax source and an expenditure burden to a new fiscal economy.

Chapter 8 presents a detailed analysis of foreign-born and educated scientists in the United States, concentrating on their occupational preferences, age distribution, levels of degrees, employment preferences, work activities and average incomes. The following Chapter 9 concentrates on the analysis of scientists from individual countries. The complete sets of statistical tables on which the last two chapters are based can be obtained from the National Science Foundation in Washington, D.C., under the title "Characteristics of Foreign Born and Educated Scientists in the United States," prepared by H. Grubel, and published in 1968.

Chapters 10 and 11 contain two case studies based on entirely different sets of raw data, the nature of which is explained in the relevant chapters. Chapter 10 applies the concept of human capital to the calculation of a tentative U.S. balance on international human capital account stemming from international student exchange. Chapter 11 presents the results of a detailed case study of Canada's international gross and net flows of economists, both in terms of numbers and value of human capital involved.

Chapter 6

EMPIRICAL EVIDENCE ON MOTIVES FOR MIGRATION

A study of our Chapter 2 dealing with motives for migration on the theoretical level reveals the importance of psychic income alongside with monetary income as determinants of the decision to migrate. Because of the importance of the psychic income in the equation and because data on motivation can readily be obtained through surveys the study of motives for migration has thus far been primarily the responsibility of psychologists and sociologists. In the present chapter, therefore, we will not present the results of our own basic research but will summarize briefly the available evidence from other sources.

In examining the data to be presented, two limitations should be kept in mind. First, the studies apply explicitly only to emigrants from the U.K., which is an important source of emigrant scientists, but is not typical of the origins of the immense number of migrants from less developed countries. Second, like many questionnaire-based studies, it reports only the percentage of respondents "mentioning" one or more particular suggested motivations, and the researchers' classifications of these "mentions." In particular, these frequencies are not weights or regression coefficients. The two surveys have been published separately, but the tables are taken from summaries prepared for the 1967 report of the British working group on migration, *The Brain Drain.*[1]

TWO QUESTIONNAIRE-BASED STUDIES

The Wilson study concentrates on about 500 scientists, while the broader Hatch-Rudd study considers the twenty odd per cent, whoever went overseas, of a group of 3,400 former British graduate students. It is not surprising, therefore, that the former study appears to indicate the greatest importance for scientific and professional opportunity—"working conditions," in our own listing. Other surveys and the opinions of experts who have dealt with scientists and Ph.D.'s also frequently assert that money is not the important factor in a migration. The point is difficult to test because most migrations do appear to bring both higher lifetime incomes and better facilities to the migrant.

There are, of course, many studies of migration, but few of them attempt to analyze data on incomes, distance and cost of moving. One of the

[1]United Kingdom, *The Brain Drain: Report of the Working Group on Migration.* Committee on Manpower Resources for Science and Technology (London: HMSO, Cmnd. 3417, 1967).

best known is by L. Sjaastad.[2] Attempting to study disaggregated gross internal U. S. migration, he finds an extraordinary sensitivity to distance, so that, in miles and 1947-49 dollars, it would take $106 per year in extra income to induce a migrant already on the move to migrate an extra 150 miles. Sjaastad's explanation of this immobility is that his data neglect the uncertainty and loss of psychic income involved in the extra distance; income is not the only explanatory variable.

Table 6.1

The Wilson Study of Scientists: Reasons for Emigrating to America: 517 British Scientists

	1964 Percentage mentioning
Low status for scientists in United Kingdom	—
Science in United Kingdom is demoralized	14.1
Britain frustrating and depressing	12.5
Lack of facilities in United Kingdom	10.4
Dissatisfied with conditions (of scientific work) in United Kingdom	17.5
Greater professional opportunities in North America	38.6
Low salaries in United Kingdom	6.2
Higher salaries in North America	18.0
Higher standard of living in North America	10.6
Higher social standing of scientists in North America	6.5

Source: *The Brain Drain: Report of the Working Group on Migration*, Committee on Manpower Resources for Science and Technology (London: HMSO, Cmnd. 3417, 1967), p. 69. The table was prepared by James A. Wilson, University of Pittsburgh, for his dissertation entitled "The Depletion of Natural Resources of Human Talent in the United Kingdom. A Special Aspect of Migration to North America, 1952-64." He analyzed 517 scientific respondents to his survey, of whom the majority are young natural scientists with high academic background.

Sjaastad's discovery that income differences may be overshadowed by other explanations is, of course, consistent with motivation and questionnaire studies of highly qualified manpower, which tend to stress the importance of work opportunities and facilities for research and the absence of impediments of culture and language. A rather special version of this finding is set out in R. G. Myers' Ph.D. thesis in which he investigates the differences in foreign students' non-returns from study in the U. S., by country of origin. It is found that no-return rates are positively correlated with the level of per capita income in the sending country, though the correlation is not impressive until national levels of education, fields and

[2]Sjaastad, "Costs and Returns to Human Migration."

types of immigration status are also considered. However, this is a surprising finding on incomes alone; it suggests that the *smaller* the differential between national and U. S. per capita income, the greater the tendency of nationals to remain after studies in the U.S.[3]

Table 6.2

The Hatch-Rudd Study of 1957-58 Graduate Students: Reasons for Going Overseas

Total ever overseas	678
	Percentage mentioning
Desire to travel	39
To gain scientific, academic experience	26
To gain other or unspecified forms of experience	18
To work in a particular department or study a particular subject	15
Availability of better research facilities	16
Financial reasons, higher salary	22
Better opportunities; offered better job but finance not specified	23
Dissatisfaction with conditions and opportunities in Britain	19
Sent by employer	4
Other reasons	3

Source: *The Brain Drain*, HMSO, p. 70. From a survey of the employment of former post graduate students, conducted by Stephen Hatch and Ernest Rudd of the University of Essex. The survey included some 3,400 graduates in 1957.

Myers also questioned a large sample of Peruvians studying in the U. S., obtaining each respondent's guesses about his alternative income streams in the U. S. and Peru. To paraphrase his summary of his very complex results, no firm answer resulted to the question whether expected earnings distinguished those who had decided to return home from those who planned to stay in the U. S. It was found that low social status students on grants and scholarships in the U. S. were planning to return to expected low incomes in Peru. Clearly other considerations than incomes or expected earnings were influencing migration decisions.

FACTORS STRENGTHENING THE DETERMINANTS

It is obvious that conditions in certain countries will create incentives to come or to leave. The literature has given much attention to these condi-

[3]Myers, "Study Abroad and the Migration of Human Resources."

tions because their removal would do much to reduce the brain drain. Consequently, it is enough simply to list a few of the more important suggestions.

Foreign Training

In the present context, the main significance of foreign training is that it familiarizes students with incomes, opportunities, and working and living conditions elsewhere. While it is possible that study abroad simply gives would-be emigrants easy access to their new country, many writers believe that scientists and professionals leave their home countries *because of* their experiences as students abroad. Countries which, though able to supply a flow of persons at the university or professional school entrance level, lack higher education facilities, are bound to see many of these students go abroad for their education and stay abroad. It is probable that, in some fields at least, starting professional schools at home will not only produce a domestic flow of qualified persons, but also reduce the loss of those who would otherwise stay abroad after training. (Obviously this assertion holds only if the local graduates do not go on to foreign post-graduate training. And even then, as a comparison of migrating physicians from Pakistan and the Philippines shows, foreign training cannot be the chief explanation of migration.)

Domestic Income Distribution

Each economy may, either as an interpretation of egalitarianism or in furtherance of aims and other policies, pursue policies which emphasize or wash out the economic structure of incomes and occupational status, thus affecting migration behavior. The incomes of scientists and engineers may be very much the result of government policy toward universities and its own departmental organizations. As one example, the European custom of overpaying "the professor" of each subject in a university often not only places the incumbent advantageously with respect to his professional colleagues at home and even overseas, but also ahead of them relative to other occupations and social groups. Senior men in such positions are therefore loathe to migrate, except for political reasons; their juniors, however (perhaps as a direct financial consequence) are ill-paid, of low social status, and interested in migration.

A second example is well known in the literature. Physicians in the United Kingdom, following an almost free[4] medical education receive low stipends as part of social policy on incomes and on welfare. It is possible that the rate of return on their own input is as high for doctors in Britain as in countries where doctors pay more for their training and get higher money incomes later. However, where the two systems coexist, it pays

[4]So far as fees and board are concerned. Foregone earnings are, however, still the chief cost of medical education. See Chapter 12.

students to get free training in the U. K. and then migrate elsewhere, which is what they do.

A third example comes from India. The high status and relative salaries of a few intellectuals, civil servants and scientists attract thousands of emulators from the same social classes, so many in fact that colleges are flooded by indifferent scholars and the market is flooded with unplaceable graduates. It is said that emigration comes naturally to both good and bad products of this system, frustrated by the over-supply. Note the similarity to the European professorship system above.

Income redistribution may also be accomplished through taxation and expenditure policy. Scientists who would be highly paid in the U. S. may be victims of steeply progressive income tax rates elsewhere; more generally, their net fiscal position may be negative, thus driving them out of the country.

Indeed all too little has been said about the positive (as opposed to the normative) effects of taxation on the brain drain, or on migration generally. It is frequently asserted that high tax rates drive people away, but the information comes from former migrants whose views are not completely reliable. What about *a priori* judgments from public finance? The literature of federal finance, for instance, is replete with suggestions about migration from one province to another, because of net fiscal pressure (fiscal residuum, in Buchanan's terminology). One would want to know whether taxes and public services do have this alleged effect on the retention or repulsion of persons contemplating migration, and whether it is closely related to other alleged effects, such as the demand for leisure and other untaxed factor allocations.

In particular, debates about the brain drain make it important to know about scientists and engineers, relative to other would-be migrants, whether:

(1) they are more heavily taxed;
(2) they are more sensitive to marginal tax increments; and,
(3) they are more responsive to the availability of public goods, transfers and social services.

One aspect of the welfare debate has centered on the "debt" of the emigrant to his home country—is he a debtor for the services absorbed in his youth, and is he morally bound to repay this debt? The positive aspect of this same question is whether small changes in services and repayments (i.e., taxes) would alter his choice about leaving.

Language and Culture

We have already noted that scientists and engineers are well informed about the advantages and opportunities elsewhere. Their education and background also help them to feel at home in a new country. On the other hand, it is at least conceivable that they are more sensitive than less educated manpower to the loss of their own culture, religion and/or language. Such considerations may help to explain why migration within the English-speaking world is so high, and why the much smaller migration within the French-speaking world rarely crosses over into English-speaking countries.[5]

THE TIME DIMENSION OF MIGRATION

It should not be assumed that every highly qualified person who leaves his country, even to work elsewhere, is necessarily adding to the brain drain. Far from it—the brain drain is both larger and smaller than this.

It may be larger because, in spite of its name, the brain drain is measured by the movement of people with certain occupations or educations, not by their brains or potential. For many attributes, the rankings of people vary. Thus, it is obvious that young children, geniuses or not, will not be counted as part of the brain drain when they move until they have acquired higher degrees or acquired academic or scientific positions. The same is true of adults classified as "managerial and administrative" personnel—the group is usually excluded because it contains many managers and owners of small businesses, some of them failures and bankrupts. Yet among them are also well-trained or experienced potential entrepreneurs, innovators, consultants and captains of industry. It is doubtful that statisticians would have counted Andrew Carnegie in the brain drain when he moved to the United States at the age of twelve, or Albert Einstein when he entered Switzerland at seventeen.

Nevertheless, in spite of these serious exclusions, the brain drain is probably *smaller* than current statistics suggest because of the difficulty of netting out the reflux of returning nationals. They return because of (a) disappointment in their fortunes or conditions in the new country, or (b) fulfillment of a plan to return after obtaining schooling, training or experience, or simply the pleasures of living and traveling abroad. A U. K. study has attempted to discover by questionnaire why British scientific emigrants return home, although the statistical difficulties both of locating former emigrants and of obtaining "correct" answers from them are of course formidable.

It must also be pointed out that, until retirement or death makes a return to one's homeland impossible, it must never be concluded that emigration is "permanent." All academics know colleagues who have made one or more return journeys to their homeland. They know that this process can take place at various ages and for a variety of personal reasons as well as for motives easily classified as "economic." The difficulties here are similar to those confronting the demographer estimating "average size of family" for a still fertile population. Just as parents add to their families

[5]See Michel Olivier, "Algerians, Africans and Frenchmen," *Interplay* 1 (May 1968): 20-25; and Robert Mosse, "France," in Walter Adams, ed., *The Brain Drain*, pp. 157-165.

after their first batch of children are nearly grown up, so older emigrants may begin to seek or accept positions in their homelands. Such a reflux has understandably long been visible among former European political refugees, but is also evident among those whose move was purely economic or professional. Hence, flow estimates of the brain drain must always be over estimates of "permanent" emigration.

Table 6.3

Hatch-Rudd Survey: Reasons for Returning to Britain

Total ever overseas who have returned to Britain	335
	Percentage mentioning
Family, domestic	36
Prefer British way of life	13
Patriotism, obligation to this country	6
Dislike of life overseas	7
End of temporary visit	41
Offer of a good job in Britain	19
Dissatisfaction with job or prospects overseas	11
Other reasons	7
Reasons not stated	3

Source: *The Brain Drain: Report of the Working Group on Migration*, HMSO, p. 71.

However, the most important category of returning "emigrants" is undoubtedly the group of students and short-term appointees (often post-doctoral fellows). The accompanying panels give some estimates of the Swedish, British, and Canadian reflux from this source—around 50 per cent of the emigration that might be recorded by statisticians depending on official returns such as those published by the U.S. immigration service.

WAVES: THE SOCIAL AND ECONOMIC DIMENSION OF MIGRATION BEHAVIOR

Some useful study has been made of the social influences on migration, quite apart from those characteristics of national economies strengthening influential determinants mentioned above. In particular, it is worth noting that brain drains do not seem to have been steady flows, but irregular and cumulative movements. There are some obvious reasons for this, but at the conclusion it will be useful to mention one or two pieces of research about unexpected aspects of the flow.

First, because in theory the brain drain is a response to a disequilibrium, we should expect it to be spasmodic, commencing in response to some change in the international economy's factor of goods' markets, and ending when population movements are no longer required. However, this is a simplistic and static view. It is possible to imagine countries steadily supporting the education of their sons in preparation for occupations abroad. Scottish marine engineers, Nepalese mercenaries, French cooks, Philippine nurses, and Swiss watchmakers may be examples. But such steady flows would hardly be the subjects of brain drain complaints.

Table 6.4

Migration and Reflux in Three Countries

	(a) Sweden	
Brain Drain	Average emigration of Swedish citizens with university degrees, 1961-62	198
Reflux	Average annual re-immigration of Swedish citizens with university degrees, 1958-59	75
Net Drain		123
	(b) United Kingdom	
Brain Drain	Total outward movement of scientific Ph.D.'s 1957-61	1,548
Reflux	Return of those on fellowships and temporary appointments	910
Net Drain		638
	(c) United Kingdom	
Brain Drain	Finish degrees in British universities in 1965	
	Engineering and Technology	230
	Science	460
		690
Reflux	Engineering and technology	75
	Science	345
		420
Net Drain	Engineering and technology	155
	Science	115
		270
	(d) United Kingdom	
Brain Drain	High degrees in Great Britain in 1965	
	Engineering	106
	Science	477
		583

Table 6.4 (cont'd.)
Migration and Reflux in Three Countries

Reflux	Engineering	16
	Science	152
		168
Net Drain	Engineering	90
	Science	325
		415
	(e) Canada	
Brain Drain	Canadian economists moving to or trained in the U.S., now in Canada or in the U.S.	107
Reflux	U.S. trained Canadian economists now in Canada	63
Net Drain		44

Sources: (a) Sweden: Göran Friborg, *A First, Preliminary Report ... Regarding the Migration of Scientists to and from Sweden* (Stockholm: Committee on Research Economics, Swedish Research Council, Report No. 20, 1968), mimeo.

(b) United Kingdom: Rearranged from *Emigration of Scientists from the United Kingdom*. Report of a Committee Appointed by the Council of the Royal Society (London: The Royal Society, 1963); summarized in *Minerva* 1 (Spring, 1963): 358-360.

(c) United Kingdom: *The Brain Drain*, p. 24.

(d) United Kingdom: Ibid.

(e) Canada: Estimates from Chapter 11.

Furthermore, emigration or immigration may be interrupted or prevented by war. Thereafter the migration may be twice as large as the initial disequilibrium would indicate. Similarly, a potential brain drain may be delayed by demographic shortage of people of the right age or sex. This is a "bottleneck," exogenous but otherwise similar to the endogenous bottlenecks mentioned as item three below.

Second, considering the brain drain simply as an adjustment to an international factor disequilibrium, we might expect the flow to be largest at the outset, then to diminish as the gap of disequilibrium was remedied. However, factor flows are rarely as monotonic as this because the absence of communications, institutions or transportation systems is not remedied until the first units of flow are completed. Thereafter uncertainty is reduced, communications home are improved and removal becomes simpler. (Marco Polo may move first, but it is not long till his cousins and their mothers-in-law are following.) We expect all migrations to be cumulative, at least till the disequilibrium is adjusted.

Third, an important brain drain must depend heavily upon the products of local universities and professional schools. If the labor markets were in equilibrium before the drain began, the subsequent perceived excess demand abroad will be transformed into a large emigration only after (a) drawing down existing stocks of scientists and professionals, raising their local demand prices and reducing their incentive to move during the waiting period when the price mechanism is attracting students through the necessary training and experience; and (b) expanding local education facilities, if the excess demand overseas is larger than can be supplied at attractive incomes, etc., by the facilities. In other words, the brain drain cannot become large until supply bottlenecks have been removed.

Fourth, demand bottlenecks may also have to be removed. Previous to the migrations, the countries of destination may have been "making do" with substitute skills or inputs. The actual creating of vacancies for the newly discovered sources of professional and scientific manpower may take time, as may the removal of legal, customary, trade union or cultural barriers to their employment.

Fifth, in addition, emigrants with particular skills or national characteristics may by their presence create new roles for themselves and their kind which were not foreseen by the original professionals or scientists nor by their employers.

Sixth, the countries of destination may be gradually building up their universities, industry or scientific establishments. Consequently their excess demand for qualified persons may also grow rather than be satisfied.

In addition to these micro-economic aspects of adjustment to international disequilibria in the markets for various kinds of educated persons, two particular categories of large and general flow should be picked out for special mention.

The first of these is refugee intellectuals. It goes without saying that the fleeing of intellectuals from Russia, Germany, Italy, China or Hungary at various times in this century can hardly be properly classified with other categories of brain drain. The motives for removal are entirely different, and the permanence of their emigration may depend upon the permanence of the conditions which drove them abroad. Nevertheless, so different are the motivations that the existence of a stream of refugees ought to have created some useful opportunities for economic research on the brain drain. One interesting circumstance, for example, is that some countries of destination were merely able to offer liberty, not necessarily large schools, institutes or research facilities. Hence, the capacity of *emigré* intellectuals to change the environment of technology or education should be open to study *ceteris paribus* (instead of *mutatis mutandis*, as is so often the case when a brilliant scientist is invited abroad to work in an already productive environment). A second, symmetrical circumstance is that the country of emigration may have provided all the physical and intellectual environment and facilities necessary to hold and use the refugee productively. His expulsion, therefore, may illustrate *ceteris paribus* the effect of the departure of isolated individuals or groups on an otherwise fruitful scientific atmosphere. Indeed, it has often seemed to us that the time is ripe for a wise scholar to compare science in Stalinist Russia, from which emigration of dissatisfied scientists was impossible, with contemporary Nazi Germany, whence emigration was compulsory.

In any case, it is to be expected that waves of refugees have also created environments favorable to subsequent migrations. This is not so much because the potential employers will seek more scientists or engineers from the refugees' country (indeed, the refugees may prevent the employment of new generations of different beliefs), but because the refugees may have established openings or vacancies for men with certain types of ability or training only taught in that country. An obvious example is the boost given to German and classical literary studies in North America by German refugees; similar remarks could be made about Chinese studies in Western universities, originally strengthened by scholars unable or unwilling to return to their homeland, now perhaps awaiting a stream of younger Chinese archeologists, historians, artists and literary specialists trained on the mainland. In the same vein, it should be noted that refugee scholars are somewhat less willing to make concessions to the educational or scientific traditions of their new countries, because their migrations have not involved a voluntary surrender of their own traditions and approaches, and because they have often been forced to migrate at a later age than is usual among brain drain migrants. Unhappy and stubborn, they may actually make a larger impact than if they washed out parts of their own past in making an adjustment to their host's culture. The discipline of economics can count many such scholars, from the greatest to the most ordinary recruit to a small college or government research branch.

The second category is the "wave" of educated migrants accommodating to long waves of economic development, land shortage, demographic forces and factor movements across the Atlantic and national borders. For this approach we are almost completely indebted to the researches of Brinley Thomas. Summarized by Walter Adams in his recent book, it runs as follows:

> Why, then, do we view the international flow of talents and skills in a different perspective from earlier observers? In the first place, as Brinley Thomas points out, the great outpouring of human capital in the 19th century from Europe to North America was complementary to an export of physical capital and unskilled labor. Flowing from the developed countries, it created an infrastructure in the developing continent and had important feedback effects on the exporting countries. It resulted, according to Thomas, in a progressive narrowing of the gap between countries in different stages of development, benefiting both sending and receiving countries.
>
> The current wave of migration, in contrast has moved in the opposite direction from that of physical capital.[6]

[6]Adams, ed., *The Brain Drain*, p. 3.

Chapter 7

THE IMMIGRATION OF SCIENTISTS AND ENGINEERS TO THE UNITED STATES 1949-1961

In this chapter we will exploit the data which the U.S. National Science Foundation, with the help of the U.S. Immigration and Naturalization Service, has collected and published in three pamphlets (National Science Foundation, 1958, 1962, 1965). In these sources are contained the numbers of scientists and engineers who emigrated to the United States between 1949 and 1961. For the years 1957-61 the data indicate the countries of last residence of these migrants; for 1961-62 the data distinguish the immigrants' countries of birth and of last residence.[1]

We have combined this latter information on emigrants by countries with newly available data on the stocks of scientists and engineers and numbers of first degrees in these fields granted by individual countries (Organization for Economic Cooperation and Development, 1964). In the next section we present time series on total U.S. immigration of scientific manpower, relate them to statistics on the U.S. output of first degrees in the various disciplines and compute the capital value of these migrants to the United States. In the third section we present time series on the losses experienced by some individual countries and relate these to their current output and existing stock of scientists and engineers. In the fourth section we examine the emigration of scientists and engineers in the context of general migration.

THE INFLOW TO THE UNITED STATES

Table 7.1 shows the number of natural scientists and engineers who emigrated from the rest of the world to the United States during the period 1949-61. As can be seen from column (1), the annual inflow increased steadily from the beginning of the period, reached a peak of 5,828 immigrants in 1957, and declined thereafter. While in this paper we are not primarily interested in the development of flows through time, it should be noted that the 1957-58 immigration figures are inflated by the influx of refugees from the Hungarian revolution in October, 1956, and that the period 1957-61 marked a period of strong economic growth in Europe and of relative economic stagnation in the United States.

The economic importance of these flows to the United States can best be seen by relating the figures on annual immigration to the annual output

[1] For a discussion of the shortcomings of these statistics see Chapter 5.

Table 7.1

Flow of Scientists and Engineers to the United States Number and Value, 1949-61

	No. of Scientists and Engineers			Educational Resource Cost per Student (U.S. $)					Social Value of Immigrants ($000)		
Year	Immi-grants (1)	U.S. Grads (2)	(2)÷(1) x 100 (3)	12 years basic (4)	4 years college (5)	1 year graduate (6)	Total (7)	Earnings foregone per man* $ (8)	Total resource cost (9)	Total earnings foregone (10)	Total (11)
1949	1,234	93,715	1.3	3,192	1,928	1,181	6,301	9,338	7,775	11,523	19,298
1950	1,519	115,464	1.3	3,468	2,152	1,302	6,922	10,030	10,515	15,236	25,751
1951	1,561	93,793	1.7	3,745	2,380	1,423	7,548	10,895	11,782	17,007	28,789
1952	2,297	72,646	3.2	3,898	2,456	1,459	7,813	11,586	17,946	26,613	44,559
1953	2,718	60,834	4.5	4,067	2,532	1,494	8.093	12,105	21,997	32,901	54,898
1954	3,200	57,883	5.5	4,297	2,704	1,602	8,603	12,105	27,530	38,736	66,266
1955	2,862	57,066	5.0	4,512	2,876	1,709	9,097	13,143	26,036	37,615	63,651
1956	3,790	62,534	6.1	4,865	3,008	1,859	9,732	13,661	36,884	51,775	88,659
1957	5,823	71,594	8.1	5,233	3,332	2,009	10,574	14,180	61,572	82,570	144,142
1958	5,190	79,677	6.5	6,231	3,424	2,081	11,736	14,353	60,910	74,492	135,402
1959	5,081	86,474	5.9	7,244	3,512	2,153	12,609	15,218	64,066	77,323	141,389
1960	4,326	89,443	4.8	7,597	3,624	2,210	13,431	15,564	58,103	67,330	125,433
1961	3,922	93,000	4.2	7,950	3,692	2,267	13,909	15,910	54,551	62,399	116,950

* For 17 years of school.

Source: Cols. (1)-(3): National Science Foundation (1962, Table 2); all years are fiscal; social sciences are excluded; data for 1961 graduates are estimated; includes professors and instructors. The estimates of col. (1) are a compilation made by the Immigration and Naturalization Service using occupation classifications of the Bureau of the Census. The occupations are reported by the applicants for visas; generally no independent checks are made by consular or immigration authorities with regard to the professional qualifications of the applicants. The estimates of col. (2) were supplied by the U.S. Department of Health, Education, and Welfare, Office of Education, and include "earned bachelor's degrees in sciences and engineering." The estimate for 1956 agrees approximately (within 2 per cent) with the number of bachelor's degrees granted in agricultural, biological, and physical sciences, and engineering and mathematics according to U.S. Department of Commerce (1958). Col. (4): The figure for 1956 was taken from Schultz (1961); the time series is based on an index of expenditure per student published regularly by the U.S. Department of Health, Education, and Welfare in various issues of the *Biennial Survey of Education in the United States*. Cols. (5), (6): Our own estimates, based on student enrolment and expenditures by institutions of higher learning as reported in various issues of *Digest of Educational Statistics* (U.S. Dept. of Health, Education, and Welfare). We followed in general the approach used by Schultz (1961) but made various adjustments to eliminate institutional expenditures on public service and organized research and to account for the generally lower student-faculty ratio in graduate education. The computations are documented in detail in Grubel and Scott (mimeographed). Col. (8): Estimate for 1956 from Schultz (1961); the time series is based on *Economic Report of the President*, 1965 (Table B29). Col. (9): col. (1) x col. (2); col. (10): col. (1) x col. (8). It should be noted that our social value calculations assume that the immigrants were of the same age and had a quality of training equal to that of U.S. scientists and engineers entering employment. This assumption was necessary because we lacked information on the age of immigrants and the quality of their education.

of first degree scientists and engineers of the U.S. educational system. Column (2) gives the absolute numbers, and column (3) expresses the number of immigrants as a percentage of the total U.S. output. The time pattern of the last series follows closely that of the basic statistics on immigration: the peak year occurred in 1957, at which time immigrants added 8.1 per cent to the number of scientists and engineers becoming available to the U.S. economy through the U.S. education system.

The magnitude of this inflow can be visualized quite readily by considering that in 1960-61 there were a total of 1,311 institutions conferring four-year Bachelor's degrees. That year, the foreign immigration was equivalent to the number of science and engineering Bachelor's degrees granted by 53 "average" U.S. universities. The expenditure of resources involved in the maintenance of such a number of educational institutions is quite large, but knowledge of the size of these expenditures would not allow us to draw any meaningful inferences about the "value" accruing to the United States from this inflow of highly educated persons.

Instead, what is required for this purpose is a more complicated computation of the human capital value of these migrants. The concept of "human capital" and its measurement has recently been developed by Schultz, Becker, and others.[2] It involves the basic idea that education is acquired through spending resources for instruction of the individual as well as by sacrificing the output the person could have produced had he worked instead of gone to school. Maintenance and other costs of living have to be incurred regardless of whether someone attends school or not and therefore are not part of the investment in him.

We have used the estimates of acquisition cost to approximate the value of the human capital brought into the United States by immigration. Since our concern is with the gains to the United States, it is appropriate to use U.S. prices, so that our computations amount to estimating what it would have cost to bring a native American to the level of education held by the average immigrant at the time he arrives.

The information required for such calculations comprises, first, the educational attainment and age of the immigrants; second, the resources spent on instructing a person in the United States until he reaches that level; and, third, the amount of earnings foregone by the individual during his school attendance. On the first item, because we were unable to obtain direct information, we made the assumption that the average immigrant had completed 4 years of college plus one year of graduate instruction and was 23 years old. This assumption is subject to revision when new evidence is accumulated. The data provided in Table 7.1 permit an easy estimate of the sensitivity of the final results to changes in the assumption.

[2]For a more detailed discussion of the human capital concept, problems of measurement and references, see Chapter 5.

The second and third sets of information are shown in columns (4)-(8) of Table 7.1, and their derivation is documented in the notes to the table.[3] The average annual educational cost per student for 17 years and the average earnings foregone by a person completing 17 years of schooling that year are found in columns (7) and (8), respectively. Each of these columns is multiplied by the number of immigrants and the resulting values are recorded in columns (9) and (10) and totaled in column (11).

As can be seen, the inflow of embodied human capital into the United States, completely unrecorded in any official statistics, has been as high as $144 million in 1957 and came to $1,055 million for the 13-year period. The 1957 figure was equivalent to 13 per cent of U.S. merchandise imports and 8 per cent of net new non-military U.S. government foreign aid grants for the same year.[4] Yet, while these values are a significant magnitude relative to some U.S. external accounts, they are of negligible importance relative to the size of the U.S. stock of human and material wealth and the capacity to produce current output. It is therefore not surprising that the "brain gain" has not become a major policy issue for the United States and we must turn to an analysis of the outflows from individual countries to find the reason for the widespread concern over the "brain drain."

IMMIGRANTS FROM INDIVIDUAL COUNTRIES

An exact measurement of the brain drain requires detailed statistical information on the occupational, educational, age, and sex composition of migrants to and from individual countries. Unfortunately, such statistics do not exist because emigration from Western countries has traditionally been restricted and governments do not keep records of people leaving the country (except casually, by number of departures by boats and planes). This fact necessitates reconstruction of emigration data for some countries by use of the carefully kept national records of immigration by other countries. The United States has been alleged to be the major country gaining brains, and an analysis of that country's immigrants is an important first step in reconstructing global emigration statistics.

One fundamental difficulty in measuring the brain drain is the high mobility of professional migrants, who often reside in at least one other country before coming to the United States and who often return home after gaining professional experience. Furthermore, U.S. immigrants recorded as being scientists or engineers may have obtained their professional training at an American university.

The best way to overcome these difficulties would be to present several empirical measures of the brain drain. First, we would distinguish gross and net flows, that is, the difference between emigration and immigration,

[3]Readers interested in greater details of computation are referred to Chapter 10.

[4]Source of import and government statistics: *Economic Report of the President* (1965, 1960).

where the latter may be partly a reflux of old emigrants. It is quite obvious that the net figure is economically more relevant than the gross in terms of estimating a national loss resulting from free migration.

Second, we would distinguish emigrants at different levels of education, such as fully trained experienced scientists and engineers leaving paid positions, students who have just completed their formal professional education, students who are at some level of preparatory general education, and children at pre-school age who later on show the intellectual capacity to become successful professionals. While emigrants at each of these levels represent a brain drain, the national "losses" are greater, the higher the level of education and professional expertise.

While ideally, therefore, an empirical investigation of the brain drain should deal with net national emigration by individuals at various levels of education (perhaps as added by the country of last residence), we have available only statistics on immigrants in science and engineering to the United States classified according to the migrants' country of last residence and by their country of birth. These data are presented in Table 7.2; column (1) shows the annual average number of immigrants for the period 1957-61 by country of last residence. Columns (6) and (7) show the number of immigrants for the two years 1962-63, the only period when the data were available both by country of last residence and of birth.

The absolute numbers of immigrants are not particularly meaningful as a measure of loss because of the different sizes of nations. Therefore we expressed the numbers as fractions of first degrees granted in science and engineering and of the stock of people active in these fields (both are averages for the 5 years).

According to column (4), Canada has lost a number of scientists and engineers representing the largest percentage either of new graduates of or its existing stock of all the countries. The emigration of 29.8 per cent of first-degree earners is an economically significant amount by any standard. However, these statistics are misleading in the case of Canada since they take account neither of the reflux from the United States nor of the inflow from other countries into Canada, both of which are known to be substantial.[5]

For the countries other than Canada in our statistics we do not know the size of reflux and immigration from third countries. If these are relatively small, the losses shown will closely reflect the true losses; but final judgment on this matter must await actual empirical evidence. As can be seen from the table, there are great variations between countries. The percentage losses by Switzerland were on the average 19 times as high as

[5]We have made a survey of economists teaching in Canadian institutions of higher learning (see Chapter 11) and have statistics on the national background of U.S. economists. There are approximately as many U.S.-born and trained economists teaching in Canada as there are Canadian-born and trained economists in teaching positions in the United States.

Table 7.2

Scientists and Engineers (S & E): Immigrants to the United States, First Degrees Granted and Stocks in Foreign Countries

	Average, 1957-61					Sum, 1962-63					Rank	
	Immigrants by last residence	First degrees in S & E	Stocks of S & E	(1)÷(2) x 100	(1)÷(3) x 1,000	Immigrants by country of birth	Immigrants by last residence	(6)÷(7)	(4)x(8)	(5)x(8)	By col. (4)	By col. (10)
	(1)	(2)	(3)	(4)	(5)	(6)	(7)	(8)	(9)	(10)	(11)	(12)
Austria	67	526	N.A.	12.7	N.A.	83	58	1.43	18.1	N.A.	5	3
France	82	9,692	144,990	0.8	0.8	120	141	0.85	0.7	0.7	12	12
Germany	425	5,402	N.A.	7.9	N.A.	784	679	1.15	9.1	N.A.	9	9
Greece	64	664	12,964	9.6	4.9	172	150	1.15	11.0	5.6	6	7
Ireland	45	484	N.A.	9.3	N.A.	107	68	1.57	14.6	N.A.	7	5
Italy	71	5,628	172,600	1.3	0.4	140	123	1.15	1.5	0.5	11	11
Netherlands	136	987	17,274	13.8	7.8	192	195	0.98	13.5	7.6	4	6
Norway	98	490	12,980	20.0	7.6	152	135	1.12	22.4	8.5	2	1
Sweden	106	1,213	21,327	8.7	5.0	113	140	0.81	7.0	4.0	8	10
Switzerland	134	791	N.A.	16.9	N.A.	218	244	0.89	15.0	N.A.	3	4
U.K.	661	8,557	227,250	7.7	2.9	2,078	1,627	1.28	9.9	3.7	10	8
Canada	1,240	4,156	61,300	29.8	20.2	1,159	2,316	0.50	18.9	10.1	1	2

Source: The figures in col. (1) are simple averages of the time series found in *National Science Foundation* (1962). Cols. (6) and (7) were taken from *National Science Foundation* (1965). The data in cols (2) and (3) are based on averaging of benchmark years found in Organization for Economic Co-operation and Development (1964, Tables 7 and 13, Annex 1). Immigration data are for fiscal years, stock and education data for calendar years.

For a precise definition of "scientists and engineers" as used in the OECD survey, see Organization for Economic Co-operation and Development (1954, pp. 21-24). The data were generated through a detailed questionnaire sent to cooperating governments. Discussion of the data handling procedure suggests that great effort went into making the data internationally comparable. However, it appears that for some countries the available national statistics are rather deficient and only round figures were presented. For Italy it was impossible to derive stock estimates without pharmacists; thus the Italian figures are not strictly comparable to those for other countries.

those of France, the country with the smallest losses according to our measure. The nations with the lowest per capita incomes in the group, Greece and Ireland, rank fairly high and show what must be considered a substantial annual outflow of scientists and engineers to the United States, given the size of the educational efforts of these countries. We should also point out that the Common Market countries of Western Europe are known to attract many workers, including skilled ones, from Greece and Ireland.

The facts that the United Kingdom ranks only in tenth place and that the percentage figure for the United Kingdom is relatively low, in spite of the concern that has been manifested about the brain drain in that country, illustrate the need for caution in interpreting these data. Many highly trained emigrants from the United Kingdom go to Commonwealth countries, and the migration to the United States represents only an unknown fraction of the total, so that there may really be a serious brain drain from the United Kingdom in spite of the facts just mentioned.

Columns (6)-(8) reveal that the natives of Ireland, Austria, and the United Kingdom have a strong tendency to migrate to other countries before coming to the United States. The most important countries of temporary residence before re-migration are Canada, Sweden, and France. On the assumption that the time period of residence in another country before coming to the United States was the same in the two periods 1957-61 and 1962-63, we have applied the ratio of immigrants by residence to immigrants by birth (col. [8]) to the percentage figures of columns (4) and (5) and obtained the estimates of columns (9) and (10). These estimates express the five-year average number of immigrants to the United States as a percentage (or as a number per thousand) of the current output (or stock) of scientists and engineers in the countries in which the immigrants were born. While these estimates differ by as much as 50 per cent from those based on last residence, columns (11) and (12) show that the ranking of the countries is not affected significantly, a switch by two places representing the maximum change. It is difficult to decide which of the two measures is more relevant as a measure of the "brain drain," since the data do not reveal at what age and educational level the average Austrian, for example, went to Canada, Sweden, or France before migrating to the United States.

A breakdown of the migration and degree information into the two categories of engineers and natural scientists indicates that on the average a substantially larger proportion of the annual output of engineers than of natural scientists emigrated to the United States. The data for engineers are shown in Table 7.3, which also shows the evolution of loss of talent, as we measure it, over the 5-year period. The series exhibits a distinct downward trend, which is nearly identical to that found for natural scientists. The fall in the loss rate as we measure it is due to both an increase in the number of first degrees granted and a decrease in the number of migrants. Clearly, the period under consideration is too short to permit the generalization that there has been a trend toward a reduction in the magnitude of the brain drain problem, especially in view of the fact that the 1957-58 immigration statistics reflect the inflow of refugees from the 1956 Hungarian revolution, who have resided in another country before coming to the United States.

Table 7.3

Immigration of Engineers to the United States as a Percentage of First Degrees Granted in Country of Last Residence

Country	1957	1958	1959	1960	1961	Mean
Austria	16.3	9.2	15.9	8.5	3.2	10.6
France	1.5	1.3	1.3	1.3	0.8	1.2
Germany	15.2	9.4	9.8	7.1	5.8	9.5
Greece	24.4	22.3	23.1	20.8	14.0	20.9
Ireland	26.6	22.0	11.1	7.1	10.8	15.5
Italy	1.8	2.6	1.9	1.5	1.0	1.8
Netherlands	37.4	8.8	13.7	20.3	15.4	19.1
Norway	26.6	31.4	26.7	18.2	17.6	24.1
Sweden	27.4	19.3	13.8	12.1	10.4	16.6
Switzerland	33.2	23.8	19.6	21.2	14.8	22.5
United Kingdom	25.9	21.8	11.3	13.4	10.3	16.5
Canada	60.6	45.5	47.1	44.3	31.5	45.7

Note: Source and definitions of "engineers" for both stock and immigrants are the same as in Table 7.2.

MIGRATION OF THE SKILLED AND GENERAL MIGRATION

When a highly skilled person leaves his current employment, the size of the resulting inefficiencies and short-run losses in production depend, first, on the extent to which other workers' output is dependent on cooperation with the emigrant's skill and, second, on the length of time required to retrain an individual to take the place of the one who has left. In an extreme case where, for example, the output of 10 workers always requires the direction of one engineer, the latter's emigration leaves 10 workers unemployed and unproductive until a new engineer is trained. It is clear that the short-run losses of this type will be smaller, the greater the substitutability of skills and the shorter the training period.

However, emigration would not cause such short-run losses even if there were zero substitutability of skills and a very long training period, if the occupational composition of the emigrants were an exact microcopy of the occupational composition of the population as a whole.[6] Alternatively, given a certain degree of substitutability between skills and an average training period, short-run losses will be greater, the greater the divergence between the skill composition of emigrants and of the population.

[6]We disregard all complications arising from differences in age structures, for which we had no empirical information.

In order to gain some understanding of the absolute magnitude of such divergencies in general and their relative importance for individual countries, we have computed the index shown in column (4) of Table 7.4. The index was derived by dividing the percentage of scientists and engineers in all immigrants to the United States (col. [1]) by the percentage of scientists and engineers in the total population (col. [2]) in the respective countries of emigration.

Table 7.4

Differences in the Propensity to Migrate to the United States Between Scientists and Engineers (S & E) and Total Population

Country	(Stock of S & E) ÷ (population) x 100	S & E Immigration) ÷ (total immigration) x 100	Index =Col (2) ÷ Col. (1)	Rank	Rank of migrants: (S & E by last residence) ÷ (first degrees)
	(1)	(2)	(3)	(4)	(5)
Netherlands	0.187	2.276	12.187	1	3
Canada	.348	4.218	12.128	2	1
Sweden	.453	4.930	10.875	3	5
Greece	.157	1.643	10.439	4	4
Norway	.366	3.551	9.705	5	2
U.K.	.435	2.650	6.087	6	6
France	.321	1.954	6.087	7	7
Italy	0.349	0.370	1.058	8	8

Source: For data on stock and flow of scientists and engineers see Table 7.2. Immigration statistics were taken from the 1964 U.S. Immigration and Naturalization Service, *Annual Reports*. Col. 5 from col. 11, Table 2.

The results of these computations show that scientists and engineers are on the average about ten times as likely to emigrate to the United States as are people from other occupations, the incidence for individual countries being relatively about the same as it was according to the percentage of first-degree measures (cols. [4] and [5]). A most interesting result is that the value of this index for the United Kingdom is about identical with its value for France (they differ only in the fourth decimal), even though a much greater proportion of first-degree earners emigrate from the United Kingdom than from France (the proportion being 7.7 and 0.8 per cent, respectively). This result is due to a combination of factors, the most important of which are the greater number of total migrants to the United States from the United Kingdom than from France (the numbers were 27,613 and 4,487, respectively, in 1959), and the greater number of first degrees granted in

France than in the United Kingdom (9,660 and 4,557, respectively, in 1959). These data suggest that the United Kingdom's problem of losing brains to the United States may be at least in part due to general migration rather than to specific disequilibria between the demands for and supplies of scientists and engineers in the two countries. While our findings are highly tentative, given the fact that the brain drain from Britain goes to other countries as well as to the United States, they are important and deserve further attention because of the policy implications they carry. The more the emigration of the highly skilled is simply the result of general emigration, the less appropriate are government policies directed toward holding specific professional groups. Such policies will be successful only if they create an otherwise undesirable disequilibrium in the market for the relevant skills.

SUMMARY AND CONCLUSIONS

Our analysis in this chapter has shown that the gains of the United States from the gross immigration of scientists and engineers in recent years have been equal to the annual output of about 5 per cent of the institutions of higher education in the United States. While the dollar value of the human capital embodied in these migrants represents the large sum of nearly $1 billion in 12 years, an addition of that amount to the capital stock of the United States and the increase in income resulting from it are small in relation to the large size of the U.S. economy.

For the individual countries of emigration, however, the losses from emigration of scientists and engineers to the United States represented substantial fractions of their current output of first degrees. Some countries experienced emigration of engineers equivalent to between 20 and 40 per cent of their first-degree earners in the discipline.

We have shown that scientists and engineers are much more likely to emigrate to the United States than are people from other occupations. This finding has important implications for the magnitude of the short-run frictional losses of output resulting from the emigration of skilled workers and, therefore, for national policies aimed at reducing the brain drain.

Our analysis and data present an incomplete picture of the brain drain as a world problem. First, we have only statistics for U.S. gains, none for other countries. Second, our data measure gross movements and do not show the return migration of skilled people who have gained working experience and professional training in the United States; nor do they reflect inflows from third countries. Third, the data do not show where the migrants received their education. Fourth, there are no data for the less-developed countries of Asia or Africa. Fifth, the statistics cover only a short period so that it is impossible to relate recent flows to past experiences and to gain a historical perspective.

Chapter 8

FOREIGN SCIENTISTS IN THE UNITED STATES, 1966

The biographical information on each scientist contained in the U.S. Register of Scientific and Technical Personnel discussed in Chapter 5 permitted the distinction of classes of "foreigners" by the extent of their foreign education. These classes, shown in Table 8.1, unfortunately do not distinguish between foreign-born scientists with a terminal professional degree obtained abroad *and* in the United States. The coding is based on the scientist's information as to the country in which he obtained his highest degree.

SCIENTISTS BY FIELDS OF SPECIALIZATION

Table 8.1 presents the basic data on the absolute numbers of U.S. scientists total and with Ph.D.'s only in the various fields of specialization, broken down by the extent of their "foreign" backgrounds in Classes A-C. The percentage figures for those three classes analytically are the most interesting and are presented in the accompanying charts for easy interpretation.

Concentrating first on the statistics pertaining to scientists with all degree levels it can be seen that the averages for all specialties are 2.0 per cent for persons born abroad and fully educated in the United States (Class A), 4.0 per cent for those born and educated abroad through at least high school graduation but with a highest degree from the United States (Class B), and 3.5 per cent for persons born and fully educated abroad (Class C).

The second group tends to consist of individuals who have come to the United States for a professional degree, attracted by U.S. relative excellence in the field, and who have taken up employment after receipt of the degree. These fields of relative U.S. leadership in the world are Sociology, Economics, Anthropology, and Statistics and Mathematics; the social sciences which saw such rapid development in the post-war period and mathematics-statistics used in the design and application of computers pioneered in the United States. In these fields the persons of foreign birth and high school with a U.S. professional degree are numerous both in an absolute sense and in relation to the other classes of foreign-born scientists.

The explanation for the large proportion of foreign-born high school linguists with a highest degree from the United States presumably lies in the comparative advantage these persons enjoy from speaking their native language.

Table 8.1

Number of Scientists by Fields of Specialization

Country of	All Scientists		Class A		Class B		Class C	
Birth	U.S. + Foreign		Foreign		Foreign		Foreign	
High School	U.S. + Foreign		U.S.		Foreign		Foreign	
Highest Degree	U.S. + Foreign		U.S.		U.S.		Foreign	
	N	%	N	%	N	%	N	%
			All Scientists					
Fields								
Chemistry	65,917	100	1,328	2.0	2,717	4.1	2,896	4.4
Earth Sciences	19,749	100	267	1.4	496	2.5	448	2.3
Meteorology	6,283	100	85	1.4	115	1.8	175	2.8
Physics	29,130	100	730	2.5	1,644	5.6	1,783	6.1
Mathematics	22,806	100	416	1.8	932	4.1	652	2.9
Agricultural Sciences	10,038	100	83	0.8	149	1.5	42	0.4
Biological Sciences	29,633	100	551	1.9	1,125	3.8	1,480	5.0
Psychology	19,020	100	489	2.6	538	2.8	223	1.2
Statistics	3,042	100	74	2.4	168	5.5	59	1.9
Economics	13,150	100	272	2.1	828	6.3	322	2.4
Sociology	3,640	100	123	3.4	235	6.5	73	2.0
Anthropology	919	100	26	2.8	30	3.3	20	2.2
Linguistics	1,269	100	37	2.9	158	12.5	69	5.4
Other fields	18,160	100	349	1.9	504	2.8	235	1.3
All	242,756	100	4,830	2.0	9,639	4.0	8,477	3.5
			Ph.D. Holders					
Chemistry	23,915	100	555	2.3	1,625	6.8	1,687	7.1
Earth Sciences	4,330	100	92	2.1	272	6.3	208	4.8
Meteorology	668	100	19	2.8	50	7.5	95	14.2
Physics	11,850	100	368	3.1	996	8.4	1,132	9.6
Mathematics	5,485	100	130	2.4	465	8.5	306	5.6
Agricultural Sciences	2,310	100	18	0.8	105	4.5	15	0.6
Biological Sciences	15,218	100	306	2.0	866	5.7	541	3.6
Psychology	12,543	100	360	2.9	397	3.2	168	1.3
Statistics	919	100	17	1.8	92	10.0	28	3.0
Economics	5,593	100	128	2.3	493	8.8	131	2.3
Sociology	2,757	100	95	3.4	191	6.9	55	2.0
Anthropology	830	100	25	3.0	29	3.5	17	2.0
Linguistics	750	100	26	3.5	100	13.3	36	4.8
Other fields	3,134	100	80	2.6	211	6.7	63	2.0
All	90,302	100	2,219	2.5	5,892	6.5	4,482	5.0

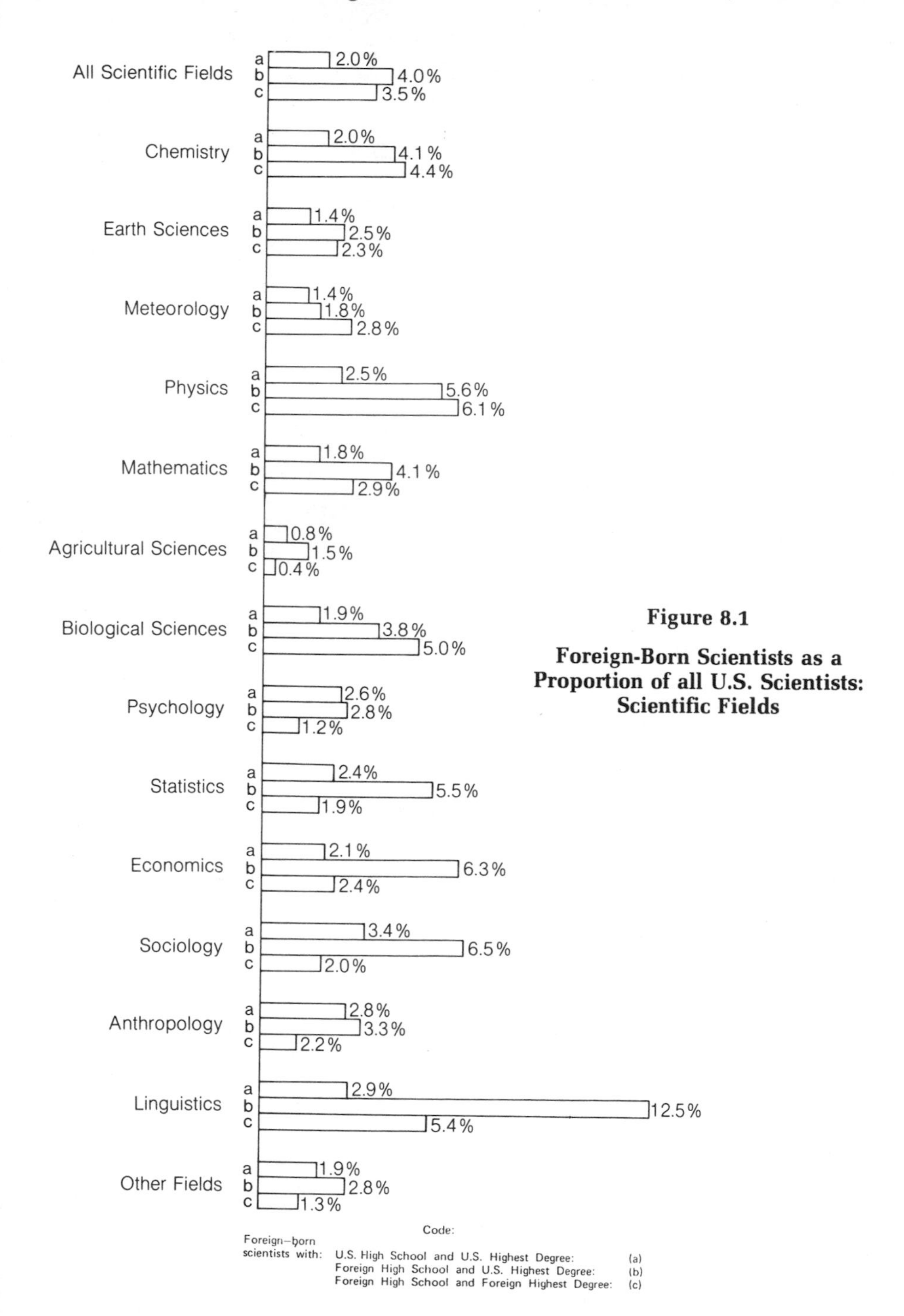

Figure 8.1

Foreign-Born Scientists as a Proportion of all U.S. Scientists: Scientific Fields

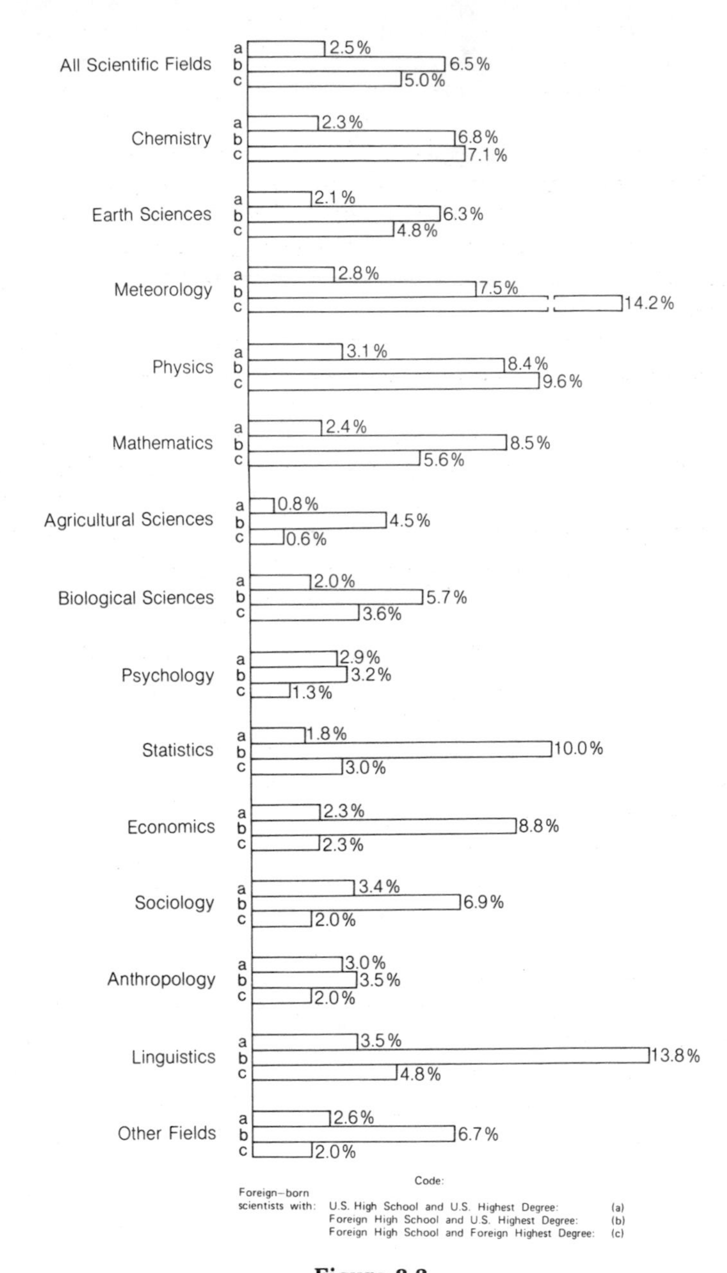

Figure 8.2

Foreign-Born Scientists as a Proportion of all U.S. Scientists: Ph.D. Holders Only

In the important fields of Chemistry, Physics and the Biological Sciences the United States leadership is not as pronounced and, relative to the age of the mature science, it is shortlived. This fact may explain why in these fields the foreign-born who are also fully trained abroad are larger in number than those who obtained their highest degree in the United States. Presumably these foreign-trained scientists were recruited from abroad when U.S. standards in scientific training and research in these fields were below those in Western Europe. This fact also explains the relatively large *levels* of 6.1, 5.0 and 4.4 per cent of the fully educated abroad in physics, biological sciences and chemistry, respectively. Further support of this reasoning is provided in the analysis of the three group age compositions presented below.

Turning now to the holders of Ph.D.'s the most notable difference from the all-scientists compilation is the greater proportionate share of foreigners in all three analytical classes and in general the more pronounced trends in fields of relative U.S. leadership discussed before. There are only two notable differences. First, in the biological sciences foreigners with a foreign high school diploma and a U.S. Ph.D. outnumber the foreign-born with a foreign Ph.D. and second, among U.S. metereologists with a Ph.D., foreign Ph.D.'s represent 14.2 percent of the total, the largest by a wide margin.

AGE DISTRIBUTION OF THE FOREIGN-BORN

Considering all professional specializations and all levels of final degrees together, Figure 8.3 shows the proportions the foreign-born represent in various age groups. The presentation reveals some interesting patterns. The first group is nearly equally distributed over the entire range of ages. The second group, on the other hand, shows a distinct concentration in the young age groups between 26 and 45 years of age. This fact could be due either to the relatively recent worldwide leadership of U.S. social sciences which has attracted students from abroad who failed to return during the last 20 years or so, or it could be due to the fact that the scientists in these age groups are in the United States for post-degree on-the-job training, ultimately planning to return home. The data do not permit the separation of these two causes.

The third group shows a pronounced concentration of foreign scientists in the older age groups, though there is a gap among those 41-55, presumably the age group which suffered the greatest mortality rate and interruption of training during World War II. The age distribution can probably be attributed to a relative push of brains from Western Europe by the persecutions during the thirties and the turmoil of World War II.

It is interesting to note that according to these statistics the brain drain appears to be taking more the form of hiring foreign students than hiring fully trained foreign scientists. Since the education of the former is most frequently financed through U.S. sources the foreign "losses" as measured by educational expenditures are less for this quantitatively most important group than it is for the group of scientists fully educated abroad.

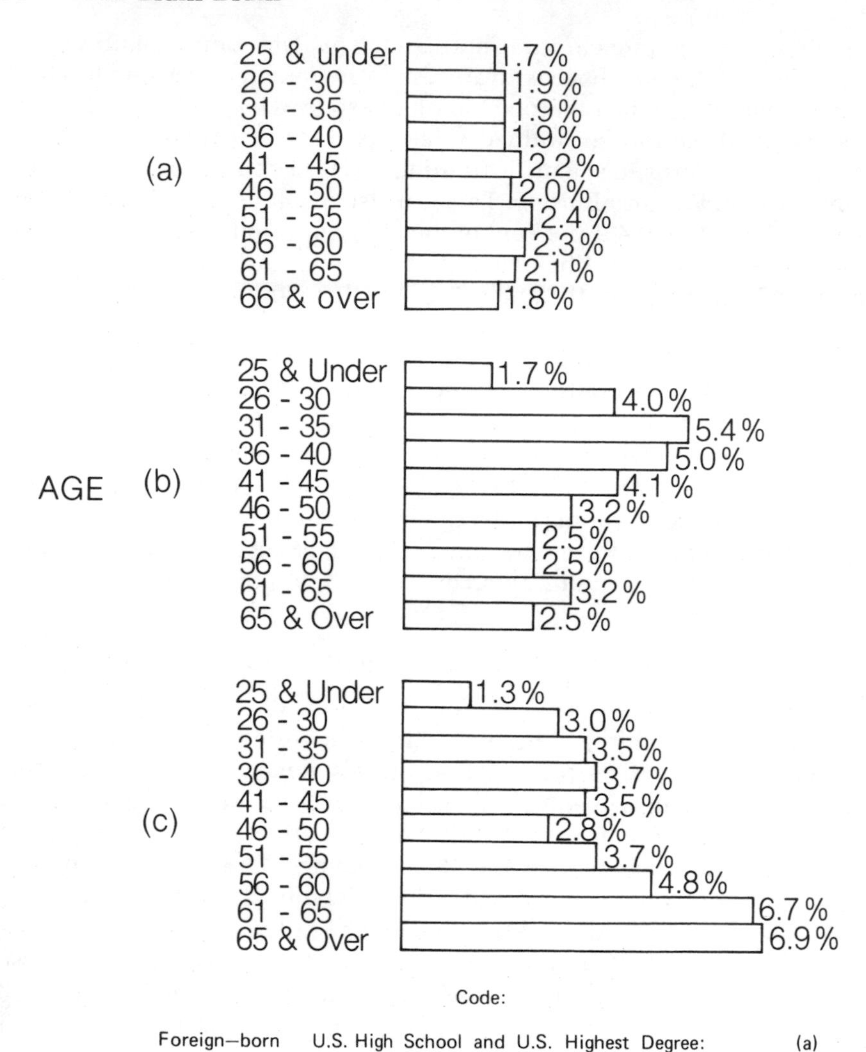

Figure 8.3

Foreign-Born Scientists as a Proportion of all U.S. Scientists: Classified by Age

WORK AND EMPLOYMENT PREFERENCES

The employment preferences of the foreign-born are shown in Figure 8.4, again broken down by the three degrees of foreign education. As can be seen, among scientists working for governments in the United States the foreign-born represent 5.2 per cent of the total, approximately equally distributed among those with the highest degree from the United States and from abroad. The next lowest employment preference is in private industry or business.

In general, the foreign-born scientists appear to have a distinct preference for academic work, allowing a mixture of teaching and research, or employment by non-profit organizations engaged in research. These facts show up clearly in Figure 8.4.

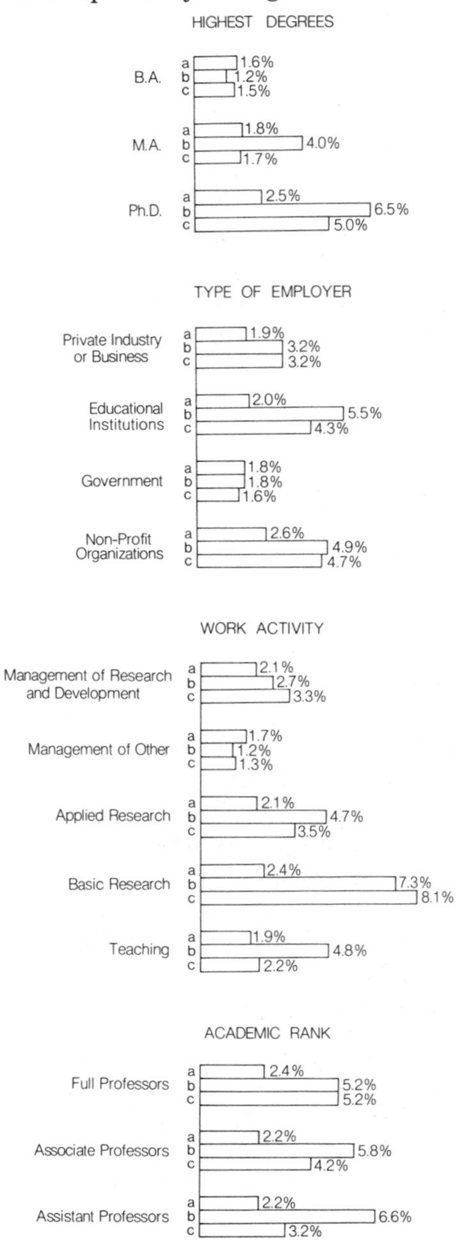

Figure 8.4

Foreign-Born Scientists as a Proportion of all U.S. Scientists: Classified by Labor Force Statistics

These types of employment and work activities have traditionally been the road for advancement enjoyed by racial and ethnic minorities since they involve fewer important personal contacts and more objectively measurable output than do activities in private industry and business. In spite of this relatively well-known phenomenon it is remarkable that as high a proportion as 17.8 per cent of all U.S. scientists in basic research are foreign. Compared with this figure, the proportion of the foreign-born in teaching is comparatively small.

Noteworthy is the relative preference for teaching and applied research of Group B scientists who have only their professional training in the United States.

AVERAGE INCOMES OF FOREIGN SCIENTISTS

It is a well-known fact that individuals' potential money incomes differ most importantly according to their educational attainments, type of employment and age, besides such difficult-to-measure factors as intelligence, drive, etc. For this reason comparisons of incomes earned by U.S. and foreign-born scientists must be in as closely as possible comparable education, age and employment categories if one wishes to discover income differences based on the more intangible qualities of these scientists.

Singled out for this chapter is the comparison of U.S. and foreign-born scientists with Ph.D.'s in academic employment, for all scientific fields by age groups. The age-income profiles shown in Figure 8.5 are based on sufficiently large numbers to be meaningful. They show that foreign-born scientists with foreign high school and a U.S. Ph.D. as a group have, for all practical purposes, average earnings identical to those of the U.S. born and educated. Another study attempted a geographic breakdown of economists born and educated abroad through high school.[1] It was found that the U.S. Ph.D. holders from Western Europe had average incomes considerably above those of the Americans, suggesting a quality bias in the selection of those coming to the United States for study, of those remaining at an American university, or both. The group of foreigners from the rest of the world with a U.S. Ph.D., which is dominated by Asians, however, showed to have considerably below U.S. average earnings. This phenomenon may well be due to discrimination based on race and language difficulties, as well as the availability of inferior alternative employment opportunities at home. The statistics presented in Figure 8.5 are the average for all regional groupings and the two biases justed noted appear to be offsetting for the group as a whole.

The average incomes of scientists born and fully educated abroad are considerably above that for the U.S. group after the age group 36-40. This fact indicates that if relative pay of persons with equal training, work and

[1] H. Grubel and A. D. Scott, "The Characteristics of Foreigners in the U.S. Economics Profession," *American Economic Review* 5 (March 1967).

age is related to ability, then the foreign-trained Ph.D.'s as a group have above-average ability. Of course, motivation and factors other than ability could be responsible for these observed income differentials.

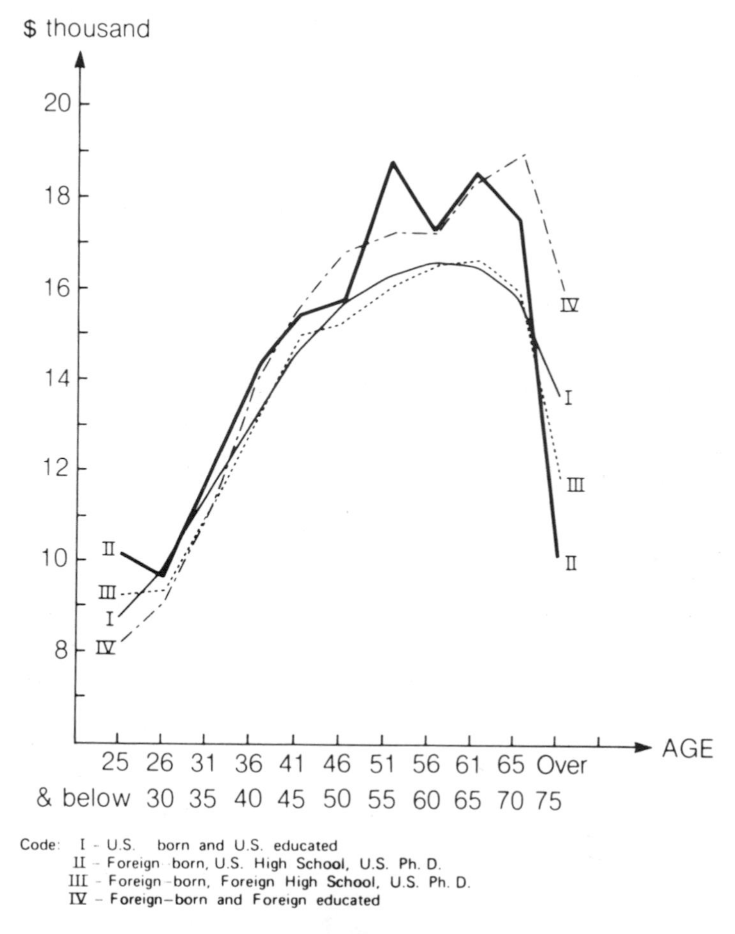

Figure 8.5

Foreign-Born Scientists as a Proportion of all U.S. Scientists: Academic Salaries of Ph.D. Holders; All Scientific Fields

As the Figure shows, foreign-born scientists fully educated in the United States also have above-average incomes. The explanation of this phenomenon is probably found in the realm of sociology and psychology. One might conjecture that a significant proportion of these individuals are the offspring of scientists who came to the United States as political refugees and that the family tradition in science aided their professional excellence.

Chapter 9

COUNTRIES OF BIRTH OF FOREIGN-BORN U.S. SCIENTISTS, 1966

The main purpose of this chapter is to present and analyze the statistics found in Table 9.1, "Countries of Birth of Foreign-Born U.S. Scientists." The analysis of the data is broken down into several sections, each of which is based on a different set of additional data designed to put the basic statistics into perspective. Section I presents the basic statistics on the stock of foreign-born and foreign-educated scientists in the United States showing numbers of all countries which have at least one of their natives working as a scientist in the United States. In the second section the absolute numbers of scientists from each country are related to the numbers of students in higher education where this measure of current effort at the training of highly skilled persons is intended to serve as a proxy for the stock of highly educated in each of the countries. The brain drain losses are examined in relation to general U.S. immigration from each of the countries in Section III of this chapter. The next section puts the losses in relation to the stock of foreign students in the United States, thus providing a clue to the magnitude of losses attributable to international student exchange. Section V summarizes the main findings.

I. NATIVE COUNTRIES OF U.S. SCIENTISTS

Table 9.1 shows that U.S. scientists born in Germany are the most numerous (3,282), followed by those born in Canada (3,097), China (2,195), the United Kingdom (2,041), India (1,382), and Austria (1,099). The ranking of the countries is changed by the count of those fully educated in their native country to one led by the United Kingdom (1,049), followed by Germany (995), Canada (872), India (378), Austria (296), Japan (282), and Switzerland (264). Holders of a U.S. Ph.D. who were born abroad are led by the natives of Canada (1,396), Germany (1,065), China (1,016), India (594), the United Kingdom (427), Austria (408), and Poland (338).

If all U.S. scientists of foreign birth holding a Ph.D. were to return to their native countries, Germany would gain the most (1,868), followed by Canada (1,790), the United Kingdom (1,236), and China (1,123).

Table 9.1 also shows that the U.S. scientists born in Central America (376; 147 Ph.D.'s), South America (545; 230 Ph.D.'s), Asia Minor (824; 393 Ph.D.'s), Africa (469; 251 Ph.D.'s), and the South Pacific (318; 211 Ph.D.'s) represent sizeable numbers in an absolute sense but rather small proportions of the contributions made by Europe (13,632; 7,518 Ph.D.'s).

Table 9.1

Countries of Birth of Foreign-Born U.S. Scientists

Country or area	Total number	No. fully educated in native country	Number of Ph.D.'s: From native country	From U.S.A.	From other country	Total
Canada	3,097	872	332	1,396	62	1,790
Mexico	159	23	0	50	0	50
TOTAL NORTH AMERICA	3,256	895	332	1,446	62	1,840
Central America: British Honduras (4), Costa Rica (17), El Salvador (7), Guatamala (7), Honduras (12), Nicaragua (10), Panama (44)						
TOTAL CENTRAL AMERICA	116	7	0	42	5	47
Cuba	244	82	46	40	1	87
Other West Indies & Bermuda: Bahamas (3), Bermuda (5), Dominican Republic (15), Haiti (9), Jamaica (45), Netherlands Antilles (9), Trinidad and Tobago (9), Windward Islands (2), Other (35)	132	3	1	53	6	60
TOTAL WEST INDIES AND BERMUDA	376	85	47	93	7	147
Argentina	205	113	46	46	5	97
Bolivia	12	0	0	3	0	3
Brazil	101	24	5	38	6	49
British Guiana	10	0	0	3	1	4
Chile	64	17	1	20	2	23
Colombia	46	9	1	13	2	16
Ecuador	16	4	1	3	0	4
Paraguay	9	2	0	1	0	1
Peru	43	13	2	13	1	16
Uruguay	14	3	0	4	1	5
Venezuela	13	3	1	5	2	8
South America not classified	12	0	0	4	0	4
TOTAL SOUTH AMERICA	545	188	57	153	20	230
Albania	5	0	0	1	1	2
Austria	1,099	296	207	408	86	701
Belgium	171	42	20	68	14	102
Bulgaria	32	3	0	12	4	16
Cyprus	23	0	0	11	1	12
Czechoslovakia	484	95	48	166	66	280
Denmark	141	54	14	44	3	61
Finland	74	24	11	25	4	40

Table 9.1 (cont'd.)

Countries of Birth of Foreign-Born U.S. Scientists

Country or area	Total number	No. fully educated in native country	Number of Ph.D.'s: From native country	From U.S.A.	From other country	Total
France	357	70	30	131	20	181
Germany	3,282	995	616	1,065	187	1,868
Greece	360	35	10	148	15	173
Hungary	789	227	96	201	83	380
Iberian Penninsula, Other	4	0	0	1	2	3
Iceland	13	1	0	4	4	8
Ireland	144	37	11	40	18	69
Italy	570	173	88	139	22	249
Luxemburg	3	0	0	1	0	1
Monaco and Malta	6	0	0	5	0	5
Netherlands	466	202	131	147	13	291
Norway	155	43	15	54	10	79
Poland	890	89	43	338	108	489
Portugal	25	5	2	5	3	10
Rumania	195	27	8	64	28	100
Spain	103	43	20	26	7	53
Sweden	149	51	28	45	5	78
Switzerland	431	264	192	87	18	297
United Kingdom	2,041	1,049	712	427	97	1,236
U.S.S.R.	726	33	13	286	66	365
Latvia	625	34	6	203	41	250
Yugoslavia	257	45	21	63	32	116
Europe, not classified	12	0	0	2	1	3
TOTAL EUROPE	13,632	4,101	2,342	4,217	959	7,518
Afghanistan (3), Kashmir (11), Nepal (4)	8	2	0	1	1	2
Ceylon	16	0	0	10	1	11
Burma	35	1	0	22	1	23
China	2,195	191	5	1,016	57	1,123
Hong Kong	153	10	1	46	8	55
India	1,382	378	151	594	73	818
Indonesia	119	5	1	31	20	52
Japan	573	282	207	172	7	386
Korea	444	56	1	198	11	210
Macao	12	0	0	5	0	5
Malaysia	22	0	0	12	1	13
Pakistan	101	10	0	44	17	61
Philippines	256	47	0	73	0	73
Singapore and Burnei	28	2	0	6	4	10
Thailand	23	1	0	5	0	5
Viet Nam	18	1	0	8	2	10
Asia, not classified	10	0	0	7	0	7
TOTAL ASIA	5,395	986	366	2,295	203	2,864

Table 9.1 (cont'd.)

Countries of Birth of Foreign-Born U.S. Scientists

Country or area	Total number	No. fully educated in native country	Number of Ph.D.'s: From native country	From U.S.A.	From other country	Total
Arabian Penninsula	5	1	0	0	1	1
Iran	174	15	3	64	9	76
Iraq	98	10	0	44	5	49
Israel	234	31	17	98	5	120
Jordan	39	0	0	14	0	14
Lebanon	77	6	0	37	1	38
Syria	37	1	0	11	2	13
Turkey	160	19	3	64	15	82
TOTAL ASIA MINOR	824	83	23	332	38	393
Algeria	9	1	0	4	0	4
Congo	8	0	0	4	1	5
East Africa: Sudan (5), Ethiopia (2), Somali (1), Uganda (4), Kenya (9), Tanzania (4), Mozambique (2), Malagasy (4)	32	2	0	15	3	18
Morocco	7	1	0	2	1	3
Nigeria	11	1	0	3	0	3
Rhodesia	9	0	0	1	4	5
South Africa: Angola (2), Zambia (5), South-West Africa (1), Unknown (64)	72	15	4	25	14	43
Union of South Africa	63	15	4	16	16	36
Tunisia (4) and Libya (1)	5	0	0	2	1	3
United Arab Republic	235	22	5	99	19	123
Western Africa: Niger (1), Gambia (1), Guinea (1), Sierra Leone (3), Liberia (3), Ghana (3)	13	0	0	7	0	7
Africa, not classified	5	0	0	0	1	1
TOTAL AFRICA	469	57	13	178	60	251
Pacific Islands: Micronesia (1), Papua (1), New Hebrides (1), Fiji (1), Samoa (3), French Polynesia (1)	14	0	0	4	0	4
Australia	188	76	49	52	26	127
New Zealand	116	43	14	40	26	80
TOTAL SOUTH PACIFIC	318	119	63	96	53	211
Canary Islands (2) and Cape Verde Islands (1)	3	0	0	1	1	2

Table 9.1 (cont'd.)

Countries of Birth of Foreign-Born U.S. Scientists

Country or area	Total number	No. fully educated in native country	Number of Ph.D.'s: From native country	From U.S.A.	From other country	Total
Indian Ocean-Reunion	2	0	0	2	0	2
TOTAL MISC. ISLANDS	5	0	0	3	1	4
WORLD TOTAL	24,936	6,521	3,243	8,855	1,407	13,505

Source: Compiled from 1966 National Register of Scientific and Technical Personnel.

The important problem with the statistics of Table 9.1 is that the absolute numbers for each country and continent do not permit the making of any meaningful statements about the relative significance of the brain drain for each geographic unit simply because of the different sizes of the nations and the different levels of human capital formation in each. In an effort to overcome this difficulty associated with the simple numbers of scientists, the ratios and rankings of Table 9.2 were prepared. The choice of the denominator was dictated by the availability of statistics on higher education. Very few countries have published statistics on the stocks of scientists or university graduates working within their borders and the only widely available and relevant data are those for the numbers of students currently enrolled in higher education. (Precise sources of the data are provided in the notes to the tables.) Unfortunately, the enrollment of students in higher education is not a perfect proxy for what is to be measured since it represents only the current effort in the creation of a stock of highly skilled persons. A country with a long history of higher education therefore tends to have a greater stock of graduates than does a country with a relatively young program of equal size. There was no way of correcting for the bias introduced by this fact and the calculations and rankings must be interpreted with the appropriate caution.

II. NATIONAL LOSSES IN RELATION TO CURRENT HIGHER EDUCATION

Each of the three groups of columns in Table 9.2 are based on the same denominator numbers of students in higher eduction, but on different measures in the numerator. Column 1a has as the numerator the sum of all U.S. scientists fully educated in the native country plus all those with a Ph.D. from the United States or third countries. As can be seen, the number of U.S. scientists in these categories are equal to nearly 26 per thousand students in higher education in Cyprus. All of the other countries in the top 10 are relatively small countries with Canada being the largest with a population of 21 million. Remarkable are the high rankings and relatively large ratios of some of the small developed countries like Austria, Switzerland, Norway and Ireland. The high ranking countries with populations not predominantly of Western European origin are Rhodesia, Hong Kong, the West Indies-Bermuda, and the Congo.

Table 9.2

Country Ranking by Various Measures of Loss

Country	(1a) Fully educated in country and all Ph.D.'s per thousand students in higher education	(1b) Rank	(2a) All Ph.D. holders per thousand students in higher education	(2b) Rank	(3a) Native Ph.D. holders per thousand students in higher education	(3b) Rank
Cyprus	25.6	1	25.6	1	0.0	-
Austria	20.4	2	18.1	3	5.3	2
Canada	19.7	3	15.2	4	2.8	4
Rhodesia	19.6	4	19.6	2	0.0	-
Switzerland	16.9	5	13.6	5	8.8	1
Norway	11.5	6	8.5	9	1.6	7
Hong Kong	11.4	7	9.8	6	.18	23
Iceland	10.1	8	9.0	8	0.0	-
Ireland	9.4	9	6.8	13	1.1	10
Luxemburg	9.3	10	9.3	7	0.0	-
Israel	9.1	11	8.2	11	1.2	9
W. Indies, Bermuda	8.4	12	8.2	10	.14	26
Congo	8.1	13	8.1	12	0.0	-
Greece	7.4	14	6.4	14	.37	18
Lebanon	7.1	15	6.1	15	0.0	-
Cuba	6.9	16	4.9	18	2.6	5
United Kingdom	6.5	17	5.1	17	2.9	3
Germany	6.4	18	5.4	16	1.8	6
New Zealand	5.4	19	4.0	20	.70	12
Iran	4.7	20	4.1	19	.16	24
Iraq	4.7	21	3.9	21	0.0	-
Denmark	3.9	22	2.3	25	.53	14
Netherlands	3.4	23	2.7	22	1.2	8
Sweden	3.4	24	2.6	23	.93	11
Nigeria	2.8	25	2.1	27	0.0	-
Korea	2.8	26	2.2	26	.010	39
Central America	2.8	27	2.4	24	0.0	-
Belgium	2.5	28	2.1	28	.41	17
Finland	2.2	29	1.7	31	.46	16
Chile	1.9	30	1.1	40	.050	33
Ceylon	1.9	31	1.9	29	0.0	-
Italy	1.9	32	1.4	34	.49	15
Burma	1.8	33	1.7	30	0.0	-
Australia	1.7	34	1.4	33	.55	13
West Africa	1.7	35	1.7	32	0.0	-

Table 9.2 (cont'd.)

Country Ranking by Various Measures of Loss

Country	(1a) Fully educated in country and all Ph.D.'s per thousand students in higher education	(1b) Rank	(2a) All Ph.D. holders per thousand students in higher education	(2b) Rank	(3a) Native Ph.D. holders per thousand students in higher education	(3b) Rank
Singapore, Brunei	1.6	36	1.3	35	0.0	-
U. of S. Africa	1.5	37	1.2	38	.13	27
Yugoslavia	1.4	38	1.2	36	.22	22
Turkey	1.3	39	1.1	41	.041	35
U. Arab Republic	1.3	40	1.2	39	.047	34
Syria	1.3	41	1.2	37	0.0	-
India	1.1	42	.84	43	.16	25
Peru	.99	43	.59	47	.073	31
Argentina	.98	44	.58	48	.27	20
Spain	.96	45	.67	44	.25	21
Indonesia	.94	46	.88	42	.017	38
Paraguay	.89	47	.30	62	0.0	-
Morocco	.84	48	.63	45	0.0	-
Ecuador	.81	49	.46	54	.12	28
Mexico	.78	50	.54	50	0.0	-
France	.72	51	.59	46	.098	29
Brazil	.70	52	.51	53	.052	32
Japan	.65	53	.55	49	.29	19
Algeria	.65	54	.52	51	0.0	-
Afg.-Kashmir-Nep.	.56	55	.28	63	0.0	-
Colombia	.56	56	.38	59	.023	37
Portugal	.53	57	.41	55	.082	30
Bolivia	.52	58	.52	52	0.0	-
Uruguay	.51	59	.32	60	0.0	-
Pakistan	.46	60	.39	56	0.0	-
Philippines	.43	61	.26	64	0.0	-
Viet Nam	.42	62	.39	57	0.0	-
Malayasia	.37	63	.39	58	0.0	-
Venezuela	.37	64	.30	61	.037	36
Thailand	.09	65	.07	65	0.0	-
Communist Bloc:						
Hungary	19.8	(3)	14.7	(4)	3.7	(2)
Latvian Nations	8.7	(11)	7.9	(12)	.19	(22)
Czechoslovakia	6.0	(18)	5.1	(16)	.87	(11)
Poland	5.1	(19)	4.6	(18)	.41	(16)
Rumania	2.8	(24)	2.4	(24)	.19	(22)
China	2.6	(27)	2.3	(25)	.010	(39)
Albania	.79	(49)	.78	(43)	0.0	-
Bulgaria	.53	(57)	.44	(54)	0.0	-
U.S.S.R.	.33	(64)	.31	(60)	.011	(38)

Table 9.2 (continued)

Country Ranking by Various Measures of Loss

Sources and Notes:

Numerators: Basic source same as Table 9.1. Column 1a is sum of figure columns 2, 4, and 5 of Table 9.1. Column 2a is last column of Table 9.1. Column 3a is column 3 of Table 9.1. Rankings with equal value of ratios shown are based on calculated additional digits.

Denominators: The number of students in higher education was found by multiplying estimates of population with numbers of students per 100,000 population.

Population Source: (a) B. Russel *et al.*, *World Handbook of Political and Social Indicators* (Yale University Press, 1964), Table 1, Total population midyear 1961. Original source: *U.N. Statistical Yearbook*, 1962 (New York, 1963).

(b) Latvian Nations: *World Almanac, 1966*, population for 1950.

(c) The populations of the divided countries Germany, Korea and Viet Nam have been combined.

(d) For Africa, population of territories includes only those countries which have at least one scientist in the U.S. Therefore, losses for continent as whole are biased upward.

Students/100,000: (a) Source: Russett, World Handbook, pp. 214-216.

(b) Definition of higher education: Enrolment in universities and post secondary professional schools, including higher teacher training. See Russett for discussion of problems of comparability.

(c) The statistics on enrolment per thousand are either for 1959, 1960 or 1961. For precise dates for each country see Russett.

(d) Where data were not available, the following adjustments were made: North Viet Nam and North Korea were assumed to have equal number of students/100,000 of population as Southern countries. Africa—small nations of East and West Africa without reports were disregarded in averaging of number for area. If no report indicates absence of higher education system, procedure overestimates total number of persons in higher education.

Of the highly developed major Western countries, Austria, Canada, Switzerland, Ireland, the United Kingdom, and Germany rank highest. All of these, except for Ireland, were also on the list of the nations which had been found to have suffered the largest losses measured in absolute numbers. India and Japan, on the other hand, because of their large populations and large higher education programe, have moved far down in comparison with their rankings in Table 9.1.

Noteworthy is the fact that of Latin American countries the losses of the West Indies-Bermuda are the highest by far (8.4), followed by the Central American Republics (2.8), Chile (1.9) and the rest of the countries at below 1.0.

At the end of Table 9.2 are listed the countries of the Communist bloc with their rankings shown in parentheses. The high ratios and rankings for Hungary, the Latvian nations, Czechoslovakia and Poland are interesting.

Column 2a presents a ratio which differs from the one presented in column 1a through the change of the numerator to the number of Ph.D. holders who obtained their degrees in their native countries, the United States or third countries. As can be seen from the inspection of columns 1b and 2b, the rankings of countries according to the two measures are very similar. The absolute difference in ranks has a value of 2.6. At the extreme, Chile and Paraguay are ranked 10 and 15 places lower, respectively, in the second measure than in the first. The absolute values of the ratios in columns 1a and 2a also differ only slightly, which is, of course, due to the fact that for most countries the number of U.S. scientists fully trained in the native country is nearly as large as the number of persons with the Ph.D. as the highest degree. This fact is correct even though a large proportion of these Ph.D. degrees were obtained in the United States or a third country (see Table 9.1).

Column 3b presents the number of Ph.D.'s from the native country as the numerator while retaining the number of students in higher education as the denominator. The frequent appearance of zeros in that column is explained by the fact that in these cases there are no foreign-born U.S. scientists holding Ph.D.'s from their native countries, presumably most frequently because no Ph.D. granting institutions are located there. It comes as no surprise that the most highly developed countries show the highest ratio since their academic training programs are the strongest. Thus, the data show that for every thousand students in higher education Switzerland has the highest number of Swiss Ph.D.'s working in the United States (8.8). Switzerland is followed by Austria (5.3), the United Kingdom (2.9), Canada (2.8), Cuba (2.6), and Germany (1.8). Cuba's high rank and ratio is probably due to the special political circumstances during the last decade. Remarkable is the low rank of France in 29th place, after many of the less-developed countries.

III. LOSSES IN RELATION TO GENERAL MIGRATION

Table 9.3 presents a set of brain drain measures which is based on the recognition that the international flow of highly skilled manpower is part of general international migration. Column 1a of Table 9.3 shows ratios with the number of U.S. scientists born and fully trained in the specific foreign country as the numerator and the number of total immigrants in thousands from that country over the period 1958-67 as the denominator.

The data show clearly the influence of U.S. immigration quotas, which restrict severely general immigration from all countries other than those of Western Europe and which can be circumvented most easily by persons possessing high levels of educational attainment. Thus, it is no surprise that the stock of Indian-born and educated scientists in the United States should equal 31.8 for every 1,000 Indian immigrants during the period 1958-67. Similarly, the figures for New Zealand, Australia, Japan and Pakistan can be explained by reference to the U.S. quota system. However, the high ratios found for Austria and Switzerland are truly remarkable, indicating that the highly educated people of these small developed nations tend to be attracted to the United States relatively more easily than they are from the larger developed nations of Western Europe with comparable stocks of educated persons. Argentinians, who face no restrictions on immigration to the United States, show a relatively high propensity of being fully educated scientists upon immigration (2.9 per thousand).

It is well known that for persons with low levels of education, one way of overcoming the U.S. quota restrictions is to enroll as a student in the

United States, become highly educated and then qualify as an immigrant under the special provisions of the law. Column 2a of Table 9.3 shows that this method was used most intensively by Indians resulting in the situation where the stock of Indian-born scientists in 1966 with a U.S. Ph.D. was equal to 49.9 per thousand Indian immigrants over the period 1958-67. The absolute magnitude of that ratio is more than twice that of Austria, the country with the second largest ratio at 23.9. Most remarkable are the absolute sizes and ranking of the ratios for Iraq and the United Arab Republic at 10.7 and 10.6 and in 5th and 6th place, respectively. Several additional Middle Eastern countries, Iran (8th), Lebanon (9th), and Israel (10th) rank highly on this basis as well.

Table 9.3

Educated Migrants and General Migration

Country	(1a) Fully educated scientists in U.S. per thousand immigrants 1958-1967	(1b) Rank	(2a) U.S. Ph.D.'s per thousand immigrants 1958-1967	(2b) Rank	(3a) Column 1a: study in higher education per thousand population	(3b) Rank
India	31.8	1	49.9	1	14.4	1
Austria	17.3	2	23.9	2	3.2	3
New Zealand	15.4	3	14.3	4	3.7	2
Switzerland	14.7	4	4.8	14	1.8	7
Australia	10.3	5	7.0	11	1.2	9
Japan	6.4	6	3.9	21	.85	12
Netherlands	5.7	7	4.1	18	.61	24
Pakistan	4.3	8	19.1	3	2.6	4
United Kingdom	4.3	9	1.7	34	.93	11
Belgium	4.1	10	6.7	12	.77	15
Denmark	3.9	11	3.2	25	.69	19
U. of South Africa	3.9	12	4.2	17	2.1	6
Germany	3.8	13	4.1	19	.77	16
Finland	3.6	14	3.7	22	.68	20
Argentina	2.9	15	1.2	36	.35	31
Canada	2.8	16	4.5	16	.43	28
Korea	2.6	17	9.2	7	.66	21
Sweden	2.5	18	2.2	28	.63	23
Iraq	2.4	19	10.7	5	1.4	8
U. Arab Republic	2.4	20	10.6	6	.60	26
Israel	2.3	21	7.3	10	.35	32
Iran	2.1	22	9.0	8	2.3	5
Norway	2.0	23	2.5	27	.78	14
Spain	2.0	24	1.2	35	.76	17
France	1.8	25	3.3	23	.27	35
Turkey	1.6	26	5.5	13	.64	27
Chile	1.5	27	1.8	32	.60	25

Table 9.3 (Cont'd.)

Educated Migrants and General Migration

Country	(1a) Fully educated scientists in U.S per thousand immigrants 1958-1967	(1b) Rank	(2a) U.S. Ph.D.'s per thousand immigrants 1958-1967	(2b) Rank	(3a) Column 1a: study in higher education per thousand population	(3b) Rank
Yugoslavia	1.4	28	2.0	30	.27	34
Brazil	1.3	29	2.1	29	.99	10
Lebanon	1.3	30	7.7	9	.36	30
Philippines	1.2	31	1.8	33	.12	41
Italy	.91	32	.73	37	.25	36
Peru	.71	33	.71	38	.28	33
Hong Kong	.70	34	3.2	24	.40	29
Greece	.64	35	2.7	26	.20	38
Ireland	.60	36	.65	39	.16	39
Viet Nam	.59	37	4.7	15	.71	18
Cuba	.53	38	.26	44	.21	37
Syria	.37	39	4.1	20	.17	40
Venezuela	.34	40	.57	41	.10	42
Morocco	.32	41	.65	40	.81	13
Indonesia	.32	42	2.0	31	.51	27
Colombia	.16	43	.23	45	.06	45
Ecuador	.14	44	.11	47	.07	43
Portugal	.10	45	.10	48	.04	46
Central America	.09	46	.56	42	.06	44
Mexico	.06	47	.13	46	.02	48
West Indies-Bermuda	.02	48	.39	43	.03	47
Communist Bloc Countries:						
Czechoslovakia	4.9	(7)	8.6	(8)	1.2	(8)
Hungary	4.5	(8)	4.0	(20)	1.7	(7)
China	2.9	(15)	15.2	(3)	4.1	(1)
Rumania	2.1	(22)	4.9	(13)	.9	(11)
U.S.S.R.	1.6	(25)	14.2	(4)	.3	(32)
Poland	1.1	(31)	4.1	(18)	.3	(32)

Source: "Statistics on Immigration 1958-67" from U.S. Department of Justice, *Annual Report 1967*, p. 61. Other data same as for Table 9.2.

Column 3a of Table 9.3 introduces a measure designed to indicate the extent to which the proportion of highly educated persons among all immigrants differs from the proportion highly educated persons represent among the total population of the migrant's native countries. For this reason the numbers of column 1a were divided by the number of students in higher education per thousand population. Unfortunately, the resultant absolute figures in column 3a are difficult to interpret. However, the meaning of the measure can be appreciated by assuming for a moment that the numerator represents the actual percentage of highly educated persons in general migration and the denominator represents the percentage of highly educated persons in the total population. Under these assumptions the figure 14.4 for India means that persons with high levels of education have been 14.4 times as likely to emigrate to the United States as have been persons with lower educational attainment.

While the actual data used to compute the statistics in column 3a are only imperfect proxies for the data which permit this clear-cut interpretation to be made the intercountry comparisons of the statistics are valid because the same proxies were used for each country. Thus, it can be seen that the large, less developed countries with low immigration quotas, India and Pakistan, rank very highly in first and fourth places respectively. Surprising are the high rankings of the small developed countries with high immigration quotas, Austria (3rd) and Switzerland (7th). Despite Iran's rank in column 1a in the low 22nd place, that country's relatively small effort in domestic higher education resulted in a 5th place in the ranking according to column 3a.

It is also of extreme interest to note that Germany, Canada, and the United Kingdom, which ranked at the very top of the list in Table 8.1 and according to absolute numbers of highly educated immigrants, rank rather low in column 3a, i.e., 16th, 11th, and 28th respectively. This finding implies that these countries' losses of highly educated persons to the United States are explained to a large extent by the magnitude of general migration and would probably be reduced significantly if total migration to the United States were curtailed.

IV. LOSSES IN RELATION TO FOREIGN STUDENT POPULATION

The statistics of Table 9.4 shed some light on the problem of non-returning foreign students studying in the United States. The ratio shown uses the stock of foreign-born scientists with a U.S. Ph.D. in the year 1966 as the numerator and the stock of foreign college students during the academic year 1963-1964 in the United States as the denominator.

Unfortunately, the U.S. Ph.D. holders include unknown numbers of persons who did not come to the United States as foreign students but as the children of immigrants. Probably the figures for Austria and Germany are inflated as a result of this fact since during the 1930s many intellectuals with a family tradition for higher education left these countries in the wake of political persecutions. The high ratios for Austria and Germany, indicating a strong propensity of students from these nations not to return home after receipt of a U.S. Ph.D., therefore must be interpreted with caution.

For the remaining countries, however, it is interesting to note that the top 17 are all well developed with the exception of Yugoslavia and that all of the less developed nations show relatively low ratios. The low value and ranking of India's (.093, in 22nd place) and Pakistan's (.045, in 41st place)

Table 9.4

Foreign Students and U.S. Ph.D. Holders

Country	Holders of U.S. Ph.D. per foreign student in U.S. 1963-64	Country	Holders of U.S. Ph.D. per foreign student in U.S. 1963-64
Austria	2.4	Chile	.050
Germany	.84	Iraq	.049
Belgium	.34	Algeria	.048
Netherlands	.34	U. of South Africa	.047
Yugoslavia	.32	Uruguay	.045
Switzerland	.31	Pakistan	.045
Denmark	.24	Indonesia	.043
United Kingdom	.24	Portugal	.041
South Africa	.24	Mexico	.038
Italy	.23	Congo	.037
Ireland	.22	Philippines	.032
New Zealand	.21	Malayasia	.027
Sweden	.19	Syria	.027
France	.17	Morocco	.026
Canada	.17	West Indies-Bermuda	.026
Finland	.15	Central America	.024
Burma	.14	Jordan	020
Luxemburg	.13	Iran	.020
Norway	.12	Peru	.020
Ceylon	.099	Viet Nam	.019
Greece	.095	Cuba	.018
India	.093	Tunisia-Libya	.018
Argentina	.090	Paraguay	.015
Iceland	.089	Hong Kong	.015
Australia	.088	Colombia	.013
Cyprus	.083	Bolivia	.012
Korea	.082	Ecuador	.011
U. Arab Republic	.081	Br. Guyana	.010
Israel	.071	West Africa	.009
Spain	.067	East Africa	.009
Turkey	.060	Rhodesia	.006
Brazil	.056	Venezuela	.004
Lebanon	.056	Afgan.-Kash.-Nepal	.004
Japan	.053	Thailand	.004
		Nigeria	.003

Source: *Open Doors*, 1964, for numbers of Foreign Students, Table 1 for numbers of Holders of U.S. Ph.D's.

ratio comes somewhat as a surprise in view of the large ratios and high ranks of these countries on the basis of the measure in Column 2a, Table 9.3 which is the proportion of U.S. Ph.D.'s in general immigration. This finding suggests that while a U.S. Ph.D. is an important method of becoming an immigrant to the United States for Indians and Pakistanis, it is so for only a relatively small proportion of students in the United States from these countries.

In general, the calculations presented in Table 9.4 lend support to the view that the non-return of foreign students holding a U.S. Ph.D. quantitatively may be an important problem. Thus, for every 100 college students from Belgium and the Netherlands studying in the United States in 1963, there is a stock of 34 natives from these countries holding U.S. Ph.D.'s. While the figures are considerably lower for most of the less developed countries, they are still significant. For example, there are 93 Indian U.S. Ph.D. holders in the United States for every 1,000 foreign students. For natives of African countries, presumably of the Negro race, on the other hand, the numbers are quite small at below 9 per thousand.

It should be noted that the stock of U.S. Ph.D. holders born abroad, estimated from the National Register of Scientific and Technical Personnel, includes an unknown number of persons who are completing their professional training in the United States through quasi-apprenticeship as post-doctoral fellows, instructors or even assistant professors. Tracing of individuals through time by the combination of subsequent Registers may provide estimates of the size of this group.

V. *SUMMARY AND CONCLUSIONS*

The present chapter contains hitherto unavailable statistics on the stock of foreign-born scientists in the United States. Table 9.1 presents for all relevant countries the numbers of U.S. scientists born in each, fully educated in each, and the numbers of those with Ph.D.'s from native universities, the United States and other countries. The statistics reveal that in all of these categories Germany, Canada, the United Kingdom, China, India and Austria have been the largest contributors to U.S. science manpower.

These simple numbers of persons are put into perspective first by the calculation of statistics which give proper weight to the differing stocks of calculated manpower in the countries of emigration. Using the number of students in higher education as a proxy for this stock it is found that the number of scientists in the United States born in Cyprus, Austria, Canada, Rhodesia and Switzerland represent the largest proportion of the number of students enrolled in higher education in these countries. The data reveal that by this measure of loss most of the less developed countries of Asia, Africa, and South America rank rather low.

A second set of calculations puts the stock of foreign-born U.S. scientists in relation to general U.S. immigration during the period 1958-67. It shows that the 1966 stock of U.S. scientists fully educated in India is equal to 31.8 per thousand Indian immigrants during that period. This figure is nearly twice as large as that for the country ranking next, Austria. It is interesting to note that the emigration propensity of Austrian and Swiss natives with high levels of education is very strong as compared with that found for other countries of equally large U.S. immigration quotas and levels of domestic human capital formation. Moreover, it appears that the large absolute numbers of U.S. scientists from Germany, the United Kingdom and Canada are at least in part explained by large general migration to, rather than the particularly strong propensity of highly educated persons to work in, the United States.

Finally, the basic statistics of Table 9.1 are used to obtain some empirical judgments on the relationship of foreign-born scientists holding a U.S. Ph.D. and working in the United States with the size of foreign student populations. It is seen that on the basis of this measure the 1966 stocks of U.S. Ph.D. holders from Austria, Germany, Belgium and the Netherlands represent the largest fraction of the stock of students from their native countries in 1963. The less developed countries of Asia, Africa and South America show small proportions and rank very low on the basis of this measure.

Chapter 10

THE COST OF U.S. COLLEGE STUDENT EXCHANGE PROGRAMS

I. INTRODUCTION

The international exchange of college students has grown rapidly in recent years. Between the academic years 1954-55 and 1963-64 the number of foreigners studying at American universities increased from 34,032 to 74,814, while the number of American college students abroad rose from 9,454 to 17,162.[1]

There seems to be widespread agreement about the range of benefits accruing to the individual students, to the academic host institutions, and to the participating countries through the exchange programs. The student's intellectual development is promoted by his contact with foreign cultures, his new social environment, and the instructional variety. The social and intellectual life on the campuses receiving foreign students is stimulated, which in turn enriches the educational experience of the domestic students. The countries from which the students come benefit both from the general development of the students and from the special skills they acquire. And, finally, the transfer of knowledge and of techniques of teaching and research made possible by the exchange programs may be very important in the development of countries now engaged in efforts of industrialization.

There are costs, however, in acquiring these largely immeasurable benefits, involving the expenditure of resources in carrying out the programs and the "wastages" arising from some students' decisions not to return to their native countries. Any rational process of deciding on the size of the U.S. foreign student exchange must therefore take into account both the costs and benefits and strike an appropriate balance between them, especially to the extent that the programs are fostered by government subsidies.

The aim of this chapter is to estimate the social resource cost to the U.S. of its engagement in a world-wide foreign college student program. Such an estimate is not now available and, as we shall see, is not easy to make. The resource value represented by human education is difficult to calculate, since education has no capitalized market value and is not included in international balance of payments statistics. In addition, estimates of the cost of numerous official and private programs, such as that under the Fulbright-Hayes Act, are so diverse that it is nearly impossible to reconcile

[1]Institute for International Education, *Open Doors* (New York, various issues).

the relevant information. In this study, we shall approach the problem by using available information on the number of foreign students, their sources of support, the average cost of education for all students in the U.S., and other information which will be presented below.

One important task of estimation involves the "value" to be attached to a student's failure to return to his native country. This problem is one which not only has economic meaning, but can be measured in terms of dollars and compared with other dollar magnitudes. The extent to which the loss of an educated individual through emigration represents a loss to his country, and the precise nature of this loss, are discussed in detail in section I. In the present inquiry we shall present two methods of estimating the dollar value of the U.S. gain from receiving an educated immigrant —our preoccupation with American gains being forced upon us by the necessity of working with American price data.

Efforts have been made both by the U.S. and by their native countries to prevent non-returning students from remaining in America after their studies are completed. These efforts have not been completely successful and perhaps never will be, because rigid enforcement would require a use of totalitarian methods and a disregard of personal welfare which are incompatible with the ideals of Western culture. The alternative to such rigid laws is a continuing effort to keep non-returnees to a minimum, while at the same time considering the actual non-returnees as a part of the cost of the program, just as automobile accidents are an unfortunate but unavoidable cost of automobile traffic. Countries make every effort to keep the frequency of accidents down, but they are unwilling either to abandon automobile traffic altogether or to limit its free circulation to the extent necessary to eliminate accidents. Beyond this, however, the parallel with automobile traffic fails; for while no one benefits from an accident, the non-returning students both gain personally and become an asset to the country of their new residence, in this case the U.S.

Our use of aggregate statistics and general expenditure estimates forces us to disregard any benefits or losses due to differences in the "quality" of the foreign students and non-returnees. Though such differences may have important effects on the welfare of the countries involved, the subject of genetic and motivational characteristics is outside our area of competence.

In the next two sections of this paper we present our estimates of the value of resources "invested" in foreign students in the U.S., and in American students abroad. In section IV we estimate the value of students not returning after their studies in the U.S. In the final section we use the data presented in the earlier sections to construct a balance sheet of the net U.S. cost of foreign student exchange. We then relate this to some other economic magnitudes in order to bring the cost estimates into perspective.

II. THE U.S. COST OF INVESTMENT IN FOREIGN STUDENTS

In an effort to clarify the nature of the annual cost to the U.S. of training a foreign student and to integrate our analysis with well-known studies on human capital, we have found it convenient to distinguish four types of cost, which may be grouped in various ways to correspond with alternative concepts of cost and value. These are: (1) earnings foregone while studying, (2) direct educational costs per student, (3) maintenance and other living expenses, and (4) transportation to and from the United States. In estimating these costs we have been forced to assume that marginal and average expenses are equal.[2]

The groupings of these costs as estimates of value from various points of view are shown in Figure 10.1. For purposes of comparison, we show in column (1) the grouping used by Schultz and others to measure domestic human capital formation in the U.S. or in any other country: the sum of (a) earnings foregone and (b) direct educational costs. The rationale for using these two categories is explained in detail by Schultz[3] and can be summarized as follows: the resources sacrificed by giving a student an additional year of education are the earnings the student could have obtained by working instead of going to school and the services he absorbs while attending school; maintenance and other living costs are incurred whether the person goes to school or not. The loss of earnings is an expense completely borne (except for scholarships and fellowships) by the individual himself, whereas the educational costs are often borne by society through publicly financed education. In measuring the social cost of having an American citizen acquire an additional year of schooling, however, both his earnings foregone and his educational expenses are counted.

In column (2) of Figure 10.1 we show the types of resource cost incurred by having a foreign student fully supported from American sources attend an American university. The foreign student's foregone earnings (a) are not considered to be a cost to the U.S., though they are a private cost to the student and a social cost to his country. On the other hand, his educational expenses (b), maintenance (c), and travel (d) represent an American outlay.

Foreign students often reduce the social cost to the U.S. by paying part or all of these expenses through remittances from home, or by working. Column (3) of Figure 10.1 illustrates the case of a fully "self-supported" student. We have indicated the existence of a residual cost to the U.S. even

[2]The reader who wishes to ponder the possible bias introduced by this assumption may want to know the numbers involved. In 1961, there were about 65,000 foreign students in the United States, out of a total enrollment at institutions of higher education of about 4 million. They included, of course, a much higher percentage of graduate and professional school enrollments than of general-course undergraduate enrollments.

[3]T. W. Schultz, "Capital Formation by Education," *Journal of Political Economy* 68 (December 1960); and "Education and Economic Growth," in Nelson B. Henry, ed., *Social Forces Influencing American Education* (Chicago: National Society for the Study of Education, 1961).

in this extreme situation because tuition charges cover only about 50 per cent of direct educational expenditures of American institutions of higher learning. In addition, we have had to assume in our calculations that all students belong either to the category of complete "self-support" or to that of complete "U.S. support," since our source of information did not allow us to discriminate between intermediate categories.

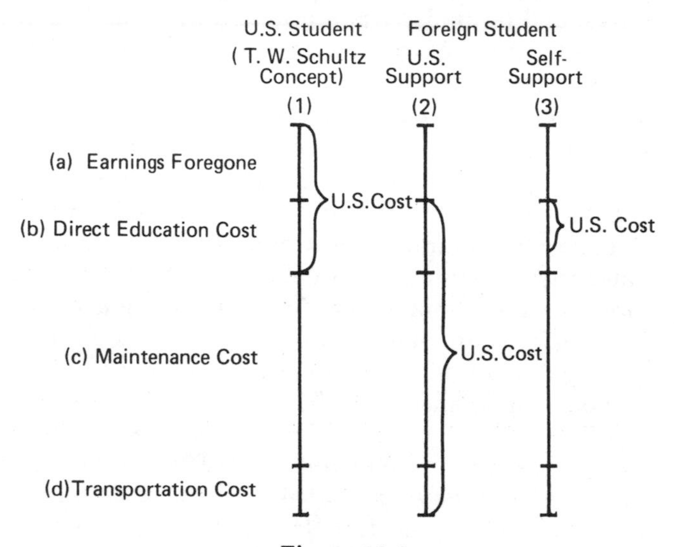

Figure 10.1

Alternative Groupings of Costs as Estimates of U.S. Investment in a Student From the U.S. and Abroad

The dollar values of the cost groupings shown in Figure 10.1 were estimated for each year in the following manner:

(a) *Earnings Foregone*. Since it was not necessary to estimate earnings foregone by foreign students in the United States, we shall postpone an explanation of this calculation until it becomes relevant later in the discussion of students who decide to remain in the United States.

(b) *Direct Educational Costs*. With two important modifications, we followed the method used by T. W. Schultz in his estimate of the annual cost of education per student for 1956; that is, we utilized the statistics collected and published biennially by the U.S. Department of Health, Education, and Welfare. Our first modification was to exclude from costs of education those expenses incurred by universities and colleges for extension and public service, organized research and related activities and sales. Organized research usually comprises about two-thirds of these non-instructional expenditures. Our reason for excluding them is that, however appropriate it may be for such activities to be located at and supported by a university, their costs do not form a part of the expense of instructing foreign students. A part of total university overhead was also pro-rated to these non-instructional costs. As a result, our estimate of average direct educational cost per U.S. student in 1956 is about $800, considerably less than the $1,166 found in the otherwise similar estimate by T. W. Schultz.

Our second modification was to derive separate estimates for the costs of instructing undergraduate and graduate students. Information for this operation proved to be extremely scanty, however, and we were forced to rely upon evidence that the ratio of graduate to undergraduate costs for "instruction and departmental research" was 4:1.[4] We applied this ratio only to instructional and departmental research costs (which we believe to be primarily faculty salaries) and not to other university costs and overheads, assuming that such expenses are uniform for undergraduate and graduate students. As a result of these adjustments, it turns out that the direct educational cost of an undergraduate in 1961-62 was only $923, or about 42 per cent of the $2,267 cost of a graduate student. In view of the large number of graduate foreign students in the U.S., such a cost difference justifies the efforts we have made to estimate the number of students of each type and the sources of their financial support; averages including all types of students might be extremely misleading.

It is well known that endowments, contributions, and public funds cover a large part of the educational expenditures of American universities not paid for by student tuition. In order to compute the cost of having a fully "self-supported" foreign student in the U.S. we have had to estimate the proportion of expenditures actually covered by tuition. The *Digest of Educational Statistics* presents median fees for undergraduates in public and in private institutions in 1962-63. We assumed that the average fee was equal to the median, and multiplied it by the number of undergraduates, thus obtaining the total undergraduate fee revenue for the year. We then subtracted this figure from the published estimate of total fee revenue received by universities to obtain an estimate of total graduate fee revenue. This estimate was, in turn, divided by the number of graduate students to produce the average graduate fee. Comparing these average graduate and undergraduate fees with our earlier estimates of the direct educational cost of graduates and undergraduates, we found that the average graduate fee covered only 28 per cent of such cost, and the average undergraduate fee only 37 per cent. While these percentages correspond to the guesses made by such people as S. E. Harris, we have no independent check on their accuracy. The lack of information on this topic has made it necessary for us to attribute the same percentages to all other years in our series.

The procedure described here nevertheless suggests that in 1961-62 a "self supported" foreign graduate student, whose education cost was

[4]Our chief source was estimates made by S. E. Harris and by B. Berelson, quoted by Harris, in *Higher Education: Resources and Finance* (New York: McGraw-Hill, 1962), p. 516.

267, drew on U.S. sources to the extent of $1,630, while he paid $637 drawn from his savings, his family, his home government, or from part-time earnings while in the United States.

(c) *Maintenance Costs.* The third type of cost incurred in the education of foreign students is the expense of their maintenance. Since visiting students are regarded here as temporarily resident in the United States for the sole purpose of obtaining training, their maintenance and subsistence, rather than the earnings foregone because they did not enter the labor force, are the relevant measure of the cost borne by the United States economy. Students who are said to be self-supporting are assumed to obtain funds for their maintenance as well as for their fees.

We obtained an estimate of the cost of a year's maintenance by interviewing people whose administrative responsibilities include correspondence with potential foreign students and giving financial assistance to foreign students already in the country. It was agreed that the "recommended" sum needed to support a typical student from abroad was $1,800 in 1955, and $2,385 in 1964. Estimates for other years were interpolated between these two dates, producing a yearly maintenance cost for 1961-62 of $2,285.[5]

(d) *Travel Costs.* For students coming from overseas, transportation can represent a large proportion of total costs. Because the item is large, we felt obliged to make an estimate of it; but, as in the case of fees, we have no independent check on the average travel expenses of a foreign student. Our procedure was to classify the home countries of foreign students studying in the United States into regions with roughly similar air fares to this country. (After some experiment, we selected Chicago as a typical port of entry because foreign students appear to be concentrated in the middle west and on the eastern seaboard, and because air fares to Chicago and to New York from many parts of the world do not differ greatly.) It was then assumed that all students paid air fares to the United States equal to the published economy (tourist) return fare from a large city in their region. For example, the fare from Sydney was used for all students coming from Oceania. Information for all years was obtained from the *Official Airlines Guide*. Because many students would have found cheaper ways to travel than by scheduled flights, our figure is probably an overestimate; however, this bias is partially offset by the fact that many students would have had to incur extra travel expenses to get to an international airport in their region. For Canadian students we assumed arbitrarily a travel expense of $100 in all years, a guess to which our final average travel cost is fairly sensitive, since about 10 per cent of foreign students come from Canada, and typical travel cost might easily be 50 per cent higher than this.

[5]This amount is supposed to maintain a student over twelve months, including typical transportation costs from port of entry to campus. For information on the subject we are indebted to the Chicago offices of the Institute for International Education.

For 1961-62, our preliminary estimate of average travel cost was $848. The average annual cost depends, however, on the length of a student's stay in the U.S.,which we estimate to be 3 years. Thus the travel cost for the stock of foreign students in the U.S. in 1961-62 would be about one-third of $848, or $283. Centering our cost in the middle year of a typical stay, we found the cost for 1961-62 to be, finally, $278.

We shall now attempt to determine who bears these costs. This part of our inquiry depends exclusively on questionnaires filled in by foreign students and summarized in the IIE publication *Open Doors*. Interpretation of this data is difficult, since the percent of colleges covered by the survey has varied from year to year. Furthermore, within the colleges covered, the proportion of foreign students giving information about their sources of support has been variable. And finally, the question answered by the respondents has not been uniform over the years, and we have no way of knowing to what extent students who claim to be self-supported were, for example, merely referring to the fact that they had won U.S. scholarships which covered all their costs. In the survey they would be morally justified in saying they "paid for themselves," but in our terms the cost of their education would be borne "by the United States."

In order to make the most of our information, while avoiding a spurious appearance of accuracy, we have adopted the following strategy: on the one hand, we have utilized our knowledge of the division of foreign students among graduates and undergraduates; on the other, we have arbitrarily assumed the proportion of U.S.-supported students to average 40 per cent per year. The data in *Open Doors* show wide fluctuations from year to year, but it appeared unreasonable to consider these a reflection of actual developments.[6]

The numbers of "self-supported" and "U.S.-supported" students were used to derive the net U.S. costs after costs borne by the foreign students themselves have been taken into account. The latter figure came to $129 million in 1961-62. The values for the years 1954 through 1963 are shown in Table 10.1.[7] The net U.S. costs have risen steadily from $60 to $173 million annually, due to increases both in average costs and in the number of students, as evidenced by our estimates of these factors (Table 10.1, items I and II).

Since the benefits from this American expenditure accrue in part to developed countries, which have large numbers of students in the U.S., it is instructive to compare these magnitudes with over-all U.S. foreign aid expenditures. In 1961, American non-military aid was approximately $4

[6]The reported percentages of U.S.-supported students between 1956 and 1964 were as follows: 41, 41, 44, 27, 26, 46, 59, 48, and 49, giving a mean of 42.2.

[7]This time series is based on annual data from *Open Doors* and on the *Biennial Survey of Education*, with linear interpolation between survey years and with the adjustments discussed in the text.

Table 10.1

Cost of Foreign College Students in the U.S.

	1954-55	1955-56	1956-57	1957-58	1958-59	1959-60	1960-61	1961-62	1962-63	1963-64
I. *Number and Type of Students in U.S.*[1]										
1. Undergraduate (UG)	20,831	21,984	24,044	26,412	27,949	27,727	29,421	31,582	34,635	40,138
2. Graduate students (GS)	13,201	14,510	16,622	16,979	19,296	20,759	23,686	26,504	30,070	34,676
3. Total Students	34,032	36,494	40,666	43,391	47,245	48,486	53,107	58,086	64,705	74,814
II. *Average Cost per Student ($)*[2]										
4. Educational cost, UG	676	719	777	833	856	878	906	923	973	1,023
5. Educational cost, GS	1,602	1,709	1,859	2,009	2,081	2,153	2,210	2,267	2,331	2,395
6. Maintenance cost	1,800	1,865	1,930	1,995	2,060	2,125	2,190	2,255	2,320	2,385
7. Cost of transportation	240	245	250	255	259	266	273	278	288	278
III. *Total Cost, All Students ($ thousands)*										
8. Educational, UG (1 x 4)[3]	14,082	15,806	18,682	22,001	23,924	24,344	26,655	29,150	33,700	41,061
9. Educational, GS (2 x 5)	21,148	24,798	30,900	34,110	40,154	44,694	52,346	60,085	70,093	83,049
10. Educational, UG + GS (8 + 9)	35,230	40,604	49,582	56,111	64,078	69,038	79,001	89,235	103,793	124,110
11. Maintenance (3 x 6)	61,258	68,061	78,485	86,565	97,325	103,033	116,304	130,984	150,116	178,431
12. Transportation (3 x 7)	8,168	8,941	10,167	11,065	12,236	12,897	14,498	16,148	18,312	20,798
13. All resources, all foreign students (10 + 11 + 12)	104,656	117,606	138,234	153,741	173,639	184,968	209,803	236,367	272,221	323,339
IV. *Adjustments for Self-Support*										
14. Self-Supported (Number), UG[4]	16,226	17,057	18,788	19,656	21,629	21,877	20,616	21,260	26,594	31,062
15. Self-Supported (Number), GS[4]	4,313	4,839	5,612	6,379	6,718	7,215	11,248	13,592	12,229	13,826
16. Educational cost not covered, UG (63% of 4)	428	455	492	527	542	556	573	584	616	648
17. By tuition, per student ($), GS (72% of 5)	1,152	1,229	1,337	1,444	1,496	1,548	1,589	1,630	1,676	1,722
18. Total educational cost net, UG (14 x 16)	6,945	7,761	9,244	10,359	11,723	12,164	11,813	12,416	16,382	20,128
19. Covered by tuition ($ thousand), GS (15 x 17)	4,969	5,947	7,503	9,211	10,050	11,169	17,873	22,155	20,496	23,808
V. *Total, Adjusted Resource Cost to U.S. ($ Thousands)*										
20. Education cost not covered by tuition (18 + 19)	11,914	13,708	16,747	19,570	21,773	23,333	29,686	34,571	36,878	43,936
21. Full U.S. support (40% of 13)	41,862	47,042	55,294	61,496	69,456	73,987	83,921	94,547	108,888	129,336
22. Adjusted total cost to U.S. (20 + 21)	53,776	60,750	72,041	81,066	91,229	97,320	113,607	129,118	145,766	173,272

[1]Rows 1-3 from *Open Doors*.
[2]For explanation of figures in rows 4-7, see text, pp. 112-14.
[3]Numbers in parentheses refer to rows in this table.
[4]Rows 14 and 15 from *Open Doors*.

billion,[8] so that the $129 million resource cost of foreign students amounts to about 3 per cent of this sum.

III. *VALUE OF SERVICES ABSORBED BY U.S. STUDENTS ABROAD*

The number of American students studying abroad is by no means negligible, though it is overshadowed statistically by the population of foreign students in the United States. In 1963, an *Open Doors* survey located 20,000 U.S. citizens in foreign institutions of higher education, of whom at least 17,000 were students. (The remaining 3,000 were U.S. faculty members, some of whom might also be studying.) The U.S. gain from having these students trained abroad cannot be estimated in the same detail as that possible in section II above, because data on proportions of undergraduate and graduate students, sources of financial support, and length of stay are not available. In the absence of published information on these matters, we have assumed certain magnitudes for them which represent our best guesses after consulting experts and studying the relevant literature. The precise nature of our assumptions can best be explained by referring to Table 10.2.

Row 1 shows the number of students abroad as reported by *Open Doors*. We assumed that the ratio of undergraduate to graduate students was 1:2, yielding the figures in rows 2 and 3. The value of a year's undergraduate and graduate education, in U.S. prices, is shown in rows 4 and 5 and was taken from our Table 10.1 (rows 4 and 5). We assumed that all American students abroad paid their own maintenance, travel expenses, and an annual tuition fee of $100 (shown in row 6). This assumption may be substantially correct in spite of the existence of the well-known Rhodes Scholarships and certain German government scholarships which provide American students with maintenance, etc. For such programs involve very small numbers relative to the total number of U.S. students abroad, and any errors introduced by our assumption are therefore likely to be negligible.

Given the basic data of rows 1-6 in Table 10.2, we arrive at the totals of rows 7-9 by multiplication. Our estimates show a steady and rapid increase in the value of educational resources absorbed by U.S. students abroad. These U.S. gains will be related to U.S. costs in section V below.

IV. *THE VALUE OF NON-RETURNING FOREIGN STUDENTS*

The cost of foreign students in the U.S., presented in section II, overestimates the American contribution by neglecting to take account of the value to the U.S. of the students who fail to return home. An adjustment is therefore necessary, requiring the following information: first, the number of students staying in the U.S.; second, their value upon arrival; and third,

[8] *Economic Report of the President* (Washington, 1965), p. 287. If the foreign aid in the form of agricultural products is valued at world prices rather than U.S. support prices, the global aid figure is $3.2 billion. For details of this estimate, see T. W. Schultz, "Value of U.S. Farm Surpluses to Underdeveloped Countries," *Journal of Farm Economics* (December 1960).

Table 10.2

Value of Services Absorbed by U.S. Students Abroad

Academic Year	1954-55	1955-56	1956-57	1957-58	1958-59	1959-60	1960-61	1961-62	1962-63
I. *Number of U.S. Students Abroad*[1]									
1. Total	9,459	9,887	12,845	10,213	13,651	15,306	19,836	16,072	17,162
2. Undergraduate students (UG)	3,185	3,296	4,282	3,400	4,500	5,102	6,612	5,357	5,720
3. Graduate students (GS)	6,272	6,591	6,813	9,101	9,101	10,204	13,224	10,715	11,442
II. *Average Values per Student ($)*									
4. Education absorbed, UG	676	719	777	833	856	878	906	923	973
5. Education absorbed, GS	1,602	1,709	1,859	2,009	2,081	2,153	2,210	2,267	2,331
6. Fees paid abroad[2]	100	100	100	100	100	100	100	100	100
III. *Total Values and Net Balance* ($ thousands)									
7. Educational Resources absorbed (2 x 4 + 3 x 5)[3]	12,200	13,633	19,246	16,519	22,833	26,449	35,215	29,853	32,249
8. Fees paid abroad (1 x 6)	946	989	1,285	1,021	1,365	1,531	1,984	1,607	1,716
9. Net foreign contribution to U.S. students abroad (7-8)	11,254	12,644	17,961	15,498	21,468	24,918	33,231	28,246	30,533

Source: Row 1 is from *Open Doors* (various issues); rows 4 and 5 are taken from Table 10.1, rows 4 and 5.

[1]The ratio of UG to GS is assumed to be 1:2.

[2]Value of fees paid is assumed.

[3]Numbers in parentheses refer to rows in this table.

the value of resources they absorbed while in the U.S. as students, which was treated as a cost in section II.

The first of these estimates came from an unpublished study by the U.S. State Department, which set the figure of non-returnees at 10 per cent of new arrivals. The procedures for estimating this statistic are very complicated since U.S. laws and immigration statistics, which have special quotas for people with skills of certain types, do not classify separately students entering on "immigration" visas (who, incidentally, are not considered to be foreign students by the Institute for International Education) and people returning as immigrants after a mandatory stay in Canada or some other country. In the absence of any other estimates, we have used the 10 per cent figure throughout. As new evidence is accumulated, our computations will have to be revised. The numbers of non-returning students, resulting from our assumption, are shown in row 1 of Table 10.3 under the year in which they first entered the country.

In estimating the value of the students upon their arrival, we assumed, on the basis of the kinds of programs in which they enrolled, that the foreign students had on the average two years of undergraduate training and were 20 years old. We used two fundamentally different approaches in computing the value of such a student. In the first, called the "earnings foregone" approach, we asked ourselves what the U.S. cost of educating an American to the same level would have been. In so doing, we used essentially the cost of human capital concept developed by Schultz and illustrated in Figure 10.1, column (1), which holds that bringing a man to a certain level of education involves both the cost of the earnings he would have received had he worked and the direct educational expenditures on him while he is in school.

Following Schultz, we assumed that earnings foregone do not start to accumulate until after age 14, so that for our students there are 6 years of foregone earnings. We took Schultz's estimate of these earnings for a person in the year 1956 and derived estimates for the other years of the period by using the index of average weekly earnings in the U.S.[9] The resultant time series is shown in row 4 of Table 10.3.

The direct education costs for the 12 years of pre-college schooling were derived by applying a per student expenditure index for the years 1954-63 to the corresponding Schultz estimate for the year 1956.[10] For the cost of two years of college eduction we used our own estimates, presented above. All of these per student expenditures are shown in rows 2 and 3 of Table 10.3. They are multiplied by the number of students remaining in the U.S., and lead to the estimate in row 8 of the total value of non-returning students as of the year they arrive. As we can see, these annual figures have

[9]The index is taken from the *Economic Report of the President*, Table B-29, col. (1), for total manufacturing. Schultz's data are found in "Education and Economic Growth," p. 65.

[10]Per student expenditure from the *Biennial Survey of Education* (various issues); Schultz estimate, "Education and Economic Growth."

Table 10.3

Capital Value of Foreign Students Staying in U.S.

Academic Year	1954-55	1955-56	1956-57	1957-58	1958-59	1959-60	1960-61	1961-62	1962-63	1963-64
1. No. of non-returning students[1] (by year of arrival)	1,350	1,454	1,668	1,683	2,735	1,783	2,004	3,220	3,730	2,378
AVERAGE COST PER STUDENT ($)										
2. Two-year undergraduates[2]	1,352	1,438	1,554	1,666	1,712	1,756	1,812	1,846	1,946	2,046
3. Twelve years of school[3]	4,297	4,512	4,865	5,233	6,231	7,244	7,597	7,950	8,226	8,579
4. Earnings foregone[3]	7,025	7,320	7,579	7,672	8,134	8,319	8,504	8,966	9,243	9,520
5. Maintenance costs[4]	22,200	22,100	22,500	23,200	23,600	24,000	24,500	24,700	25,000	25,300
TOTAL COST ALL STUDENTS ($ THOUSANDS)										
A. *Earnings Foregone Approach*										
6. Education cost, school and undergraduate [1 x (2 + 3)][5]	7,626	8,651	10,707	11,611	21,724	16,047	18,855	31,543	37,942	25,266
7. Earnings foregone (1 x 4)	9,484	10,643	12,642	12,712	22,246	14,833	17,042	28,871	34,476	22,639
8. Total capital value (6 + 7)	17,110	19,294	23,349	24,323	43,970	30,880	35,897	60,414	72,418	47,905
B. *Maintenance Cost Approach ($ thousands)*										
9. Education cost, school and undergraduate (6)	7,626	8,651	10,707	11,611	21,724	16,047	18,855	31,543	37,942	25,266
10. Maintenance cost (1 x 5)	29,970	32,133	37,530	39,046	64,546	42,792	49,098	79,534	93,250	60,163
11. Total value (9 + 10)	37,596	40,784	48,237	50,657	86,270	58,839	67,953	111,077	131,192	85,429

[1]10% of students entering the U.S. in the given year; data on students entering from *Open Doors* (various issues).
[2]From Table 10.1, row 4.
[3]From Schultz; see text.
[4]Our estimate; see text.
[6]Numbers in parentheses refer to rows in this table.

fluctuated widely from year to year, depending on the number of newly arriving students. They will be integrated with our earlier cost estimates in section V below.

Our second approach to measuring the value of the non-returning students we have called the "maintenance cost" approach. In this concept, the value of educated immigrants to the United States is not what the cost would have been of schooling a similar American child, but what the United States saved in resources because the immigrant was educated and maintained as a child abroad before coming to America. Thus the two components of the "resources saved" by the immigration at age 20 are prior maintenance and education costs. Since our estimate of the latter is the same as that already derived, we confined ourselves here to explaining the former.

The calculation itself can be explained quite quickly. In the earlier calculation (for 1961-62) of the cost to the U.S. of investing in foreign students, we suggested that one year's maintenance would cost about $2,320. If the students are 20 years old, how much would their maintenance expenses total over 20 years? Obviously, the cost of a year's maintenance increases with a child's age and decreases with the size of the family or institution where he lives. On the basis of several investigations, we suggest that $24,700 would maintain a child at the appropriate standard for 20 years at 1961-62 prices.[11] This figure is considerably higher than the alternatives "earnings foregone" per student discussed above. While the earnings foregone for 3,220 American students would be about $29 million in 1961-62, the U.S. resources saved on an equal number of students maintained abroad would be (3,220 x $24,700) or $79.5 million.[12]

Estimates of the total value of foreign students remaining in the U.S., covering the entire time period and following the "maintenance cost" approach, are shown in rows 9-11 of Table 10.3. We feel that both ap-

[11]This estimate was actually made for 1959. It depends upon three observations: (1) a student's maintenance cost at age 20; (2) the *Monthly Labor Review* (November 1960), p. 1200, estimate of the cost of maintaining a "marginal" child in the U.S. under 9 years of age; and (3) a similar estimate for a teenager. These three figures were linked by linear interpolation and totaled for a 20-year period. The 1959 total was almost precisely $24,000. For other years, this figure was adjusted by the *Consumer Price Index* to the appropriate level.

[12]The real problem with the maintenance estimate is not the determination of the cost of child-rearing, but the conceptual problem of deciding upon the appropriate period of years. In using a 20-year period above we imply that the U.S. resource saving should be reckoned from the birth of the future immigrant. This concept is rather far-fetched because the child cannot make the decision until he has information—say at 14 years of age at the earliest. Neither his parents nor the United States, anxious to recruit his future services, can be certain that he will become a professional resident in the United States until about age 14 or later. Thus a good argument can be made that the maintenance cost saved should be figured only for the period during which it is *apparent* that his living abroad is actually a saving to the U.S. Without debating this conceptual difficulty, however, we can report that in order to reconcile an estimate obtained by the "maintenance cost" approach with one computed by "earnings foregone," the appropriate period for estimating both would be about 4 years—from age 16.

proaches to measuring the value of educated people immigrating to the U.S. have equal merit in terms of their logic. The widely different results may be viewed as providing us with extreme values, within which the "true" value can be found.

The U.S. cost estimate of section II requires now another adjustment, due to the fact that the value of resources absorbed by the non-returning students was there considered a U.S. cost. Since these resources never leave the country, however, they must be subtracted from the cost estimate. The size of this adjustment will be 10 per cent of the total cost of having foreign students in the U.S., taken *before* the adjustment for self-support. By using this gross figure we have adjusted the U.S. cost not only for the resources absorbed by the non-returning students and paid for by the U.S., but also for the resources paid for by the students themselves. In effect, the non-returning students' "self-support," to the extent that it was financed by foreign remittances, is a subsidy to the U.S. and must therefore be counted as an American gain. This final adjustment to U.S. cost, amounting to $24 million in 1961-62, is introduced in row 2 of Table 10.4.

V. *THE FINAL BALANCE AND CONCLUSIONS*

The various components entering into the U.S. balance on resource flows in connection with foreign student exchange were developed and explained in detail in the three preceding sections of this chapter. We now turn to the task of combining them into the final balance sheet making up Table 10.4. All costs to the U.S. are entered with a minus sign while benefits are shown as positive entries.

The largest cost figure is shown in row 1 and represents the value of the resources absorbed by foreign students in the U.S. in the respective years and not paid for by remittances from home or from their own work. The next two rows are adjustments of this cost figure made necessary by non-returning students. Row 2 represents the value of resources spent on non-returnees and considered a cost in the calculations of row 1, while row 3 measures the capital value of these new American citizens as of the date of their arrival. The sum of the three rows provides us with an estimate of the net cost of having the foreign students on American soil. As we can see, this figure has been growing irregularly during the ten years in question, averaging $45 million annually. Row 5 represents the value of educational resources absorbed by U.S. students abroad, and leads to our estimate of the American net balance of participating in a multilateral foreign student program. The average on this final balance comes to an annual cost of $18 million.

The second part of the table derives an alternative estimate of the U.S. balance using our upper limit on the value of the non-returning students. This figure is shown in row 3a, replacing row 3 of the previous calculation. The final balance values found in rows 4a and 6a correspond to rows 4 and 6 of the first section. According to this method of calculation, the U.S.

derived an annual *benefit* averaging $16 million per year from its foreign student program.

Whichever of the two figures for the final U.S. balance one considers to be more appropriate, the importance of both estimates is that the resource cost of the program is very small indeed. Considering the high cost estimate of the two alternatives, the $17 million in 1961-62 is about .05 per cent of American imports ($28 billion), .03 per cent of U.S. defense expenditures ($50 billion), and 4 per cent of non-military foreign aid ($4 billion) in the same year. This is a very low price for the U.S. to pay for a most important part of its total aid and development effort, not to mention the more direct benefits to the American academic environment which we outlined earlier. If world-wide and U.S. benefits are as great as specialists have suggested, and if U.S. costs are as low as our last few pages indicate, a *prima facie* case is created for expanding the U.S. foreign student exchange.

Table 10.4

United States Balance on Foreign Training ($ thousand)

Academic Year	1954-55	1955-56	1956-57	1957-58	1958-59	1959-60	1960-61	1961-62	1062-63	1963-64
I. *Earnings Foregone Approach*										
1. Adjusted total cost to U.S.[1]	—53,776	—60,750	—72,041	—81,066	—91,229	—97,320	—113,607	—129,118	—145,766	—173,272
2. Value of U.S. education of non-returnees[2]	10,466	11,758	13,823	15,372	17,364	18,497	21,227	23,637	27,222	32,334
3. Capital value of non-returnees[3]	17,110	19,268	23,349	24,323	43,970	30,880	35,897	60,414	72,418	47,905
4. Net cost of foreign students in U.S. (1 + 1 + 3)[4]	—26,200	—29,724	—34,869	—41,371	—29,895	—47,943	—56,483	—45,067	—46,126	—93,033
5. Value received by U.S. students abroad[5]	11,254	12,644	17,961	15,498	21,468	24,918	33,231	28,246	30,533	N.A.
6. Overall U.S. balance on foreign training (4 + 5)	—14,946	—17,080	—16,908	—25,873	—8,427	—23,025	—23,252	—16,821	—15,593	N.A.
II. *Maintenance Cost Approach*										
3a. Maintenance saved through non-returnees[6]	37,596	40,784	48,237	50,657	86,270	58,839	67,953	111,077	131,192	85,429
4a. Net cost of foreign students in U.S. (1 + 2 + 3a)	—4,112	—8,208	—9,981	—15,037	+12,405	—19,984	—24,427	+5,596	+12,648	—55,509
6a. Overall U.S. balance in foreign training (4a + 5)	+7,142	+4,436	+7,980	+461	+33,873	+4,934	+8,804	+33,842	+43,181	N.A.

[1] Items entered with minus sign (—) are cost to U.S.; other entries represent U.S. gain. Row 1 is taken from Table 10.1, row 22.
[2] 10% of Table 10.1, row 13.
[3] From Table 10.3, row 8.
[4] Numbers in parentheses refer to rows in this table.
[5] From Table 10.2, row 9.
[6] From Table 10.3, row 11.

Chapter 11

THE MIGRATIONS OF CANADIAN ECONOMISTS

By applying to the Canadian economics profession techniques we have developed in preceding chapters, we construct in this chapter a "balance of indebtedness" between Canada and the United States. This balance arises from the contributions made by schooling in each country to the stock of academic economists in the other country. We show that, although Canada has contributed a large number of economists to the United States' stock, she has, on all assumptions about costs, gained more human capital than she has lost.

This may be surprising, because Canada is well-known as a source of American scientists and engineers, and is well-known too, especially in Europe, as the destination of scientists and managers from Europe and from less-developed countries.[1] Most of such impressions are based on *flow* data, of immigrant arrivals,[2] though some are based on census measures and special stock enumerations.[3] But all are extremely misleading, not simply through their inclusions and omissions of persons, but, more important, in their arbitrary mention or neglect of the origin and value of the human capital (schooling) embodied in the migrants. This paper attempts to remedy these shortcomings by an analysis of academic economists: the number and value of native- and foreign-born Canadians who have studied abroad[4] and returned to Canada, and of foreign-born who have joined the profession in Canada. We are able to compare some of these enumerations with similar estimates about economists with Canadian birth and schooling now in the United States. This paper does not deal with the reasons for, or motives underlying, the flows.

Before proceeding, however, it is worth asking whether a study confined to economists is an adequate source of information either about Canadian professions or about brain drain balances of indebtedness. Its representativeness of the migration rates or of foreign-born percentages in

[1]Parai, *Immigration and Emigration of Professional and Skilled Manpower . . .* , *pp. 79-83, 120-124.*

[2]For a recent summary, see K. V. Pankhurst, "Migration Between Canada and the United States," *Annals of the American Academy of Political and Social Science* 367 (September 1968): 53-62.

[3]U.S. Department of Commerce, Bureau of the Census, "Occupational Characteristics," *U.S. Census of Population: 1960*, Final Report PC (2)-72, Table 8.

[4]In the 1960s, about 2,500 Canadians in all fields moved to the U.S. for schooling. See *Open Doors* (1963), p. 5; B. W. Wilkinson, *Studies in the Economics of Education*, Economics and Research Branch, Canada Dept. of Labour, Occasional Paper No. 4 (Ottawa, 1966), Table 4, p. 60, shows the number of "students" over a 10-year period, but this is certainly an understatement, being based on American visa information.

all Canadian professions must indeed be in doubt. We have collected evidence, some of it published,[5] that suggests that economists are more apt to take training abroad or to migrate than other Canadian disciplines or sciences. Hence, our economists' sums and balances may not help to predict analogous values among physicians, chemists, or professors of English.

On the other hand, economists do provide an excellent illustration of our main point: that the existence of a larger number of Canadians in the United States than of similar Americans in Canada does not indicate that the United States is "indebted" to Canada for a surplus of exported human capital. This is because many Canadian economists obtained their graduate training abroad. Human capital is credited not to the place of birth but to where education occurs.

THE BALANCE ON THE CANADIAN-AMERICAN EXCHANGE OF ACADEMIC ECONOMISTS

In this section we estimate the values of the prior Canadian flows to the U.S., and of the U.S. flows to Canada, by examining the 1964 stocks. This procedure summarizes the situation only at some expense of sacrifice of full accuracy:

(a) The accompanying chart, Figure 11.1, is based upon the known origin of Canadian-trained economists in the U.S. and of a sample of economists in Canada. It shows the large contribution of the Rest of the World, which, however, is excluded from our balance sheet calculations.

(b) The Canadian information is based upon a sample of a universe of unknown size. We have had to guess what the total magnitude should be.

Nevertheless we think it of some value to measure the complex "debts" and "gains" which emerge when two countries as close as Canada and the United States in effect draw on the same labor market for the manning of university departments in a single profession. This is because in spite of the publicity given to the brain drain, and the undoubted fact that Canada has lost many valuable and important economists to the United States, the balance of our calculations is always in favor of Canada, the loss of human capital by emigration being in every calculation more than offset by the gain of human capital to those now working in Canada from training in U.S. institutions.

Method. The method used is substantially the same as that followed in Chapter 9. That is, we assume that each migrant, according to his age and education, embodies an amount of human capital indicated by the resource cost of his schooling, his earnings foregone during schooling, and/or his maintenance costs at certain periods before or during schooling. His migration is a "gain" or "benefit" to the country whither he moves, which is now "indebted" to the country that incurred a "cost" or "loss" where the

[5] A. D. Scott, "The Recruitment and Migration of Canadian Social Scientists," *Canadian Journal of Economics and Political Science* 33, 4 (November 1967): 495-508.

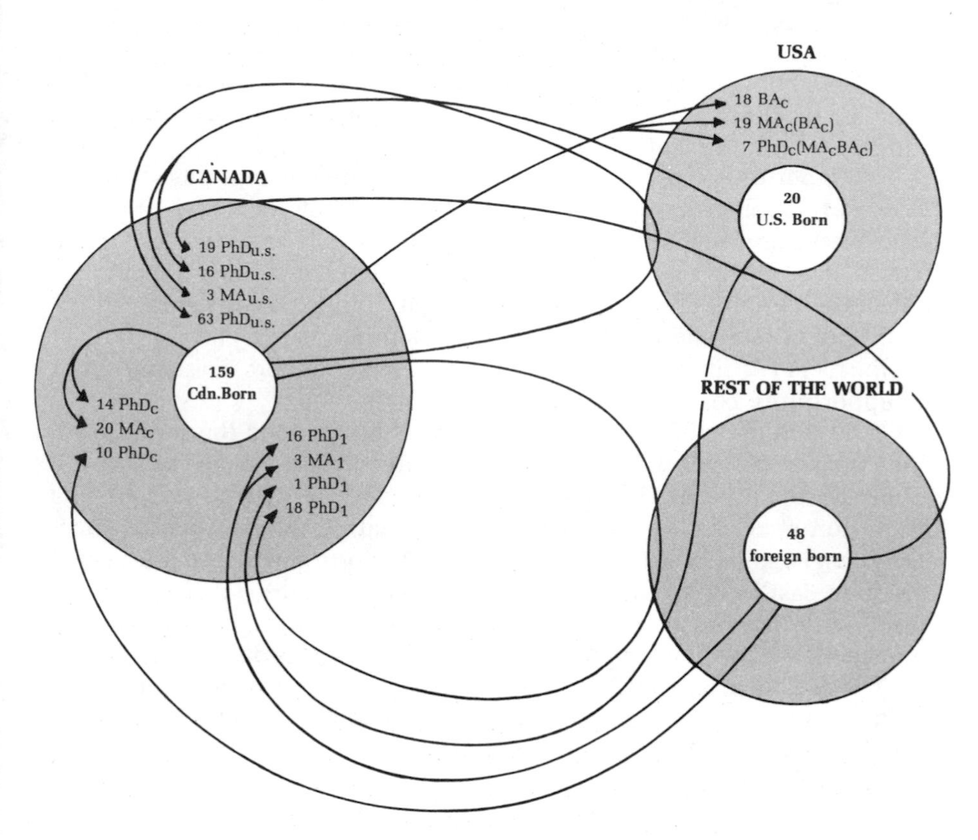

Figure 11.1

Synthetic Flow-Chart Based on Careers of 44 U.S. Academics with Canadian B.A.'s and of 183 Canadian Academics

Sources: (1) National Science Foundation-American Economic Association questionnaire—used to study American economists of Canadian birth, training or experience described in H. G. Grubel and A. D. Scott, "Foreigners in the U.S. Economics Profession," *American Economic Review*, LVII, 1 (March 1967), 131-45.

(2) A ten per cent sample of names drawn from the directory of the American Economic Association—most of the data obtained from the sample was supplanted by the NSF-AEA questionnaire.

(3) Data on salaries and qualifications of teachers in universities and colleges collected by DBS (published annually as No. 81-203).

(4) The first of two sample questionnaires sent to Canadian university economics departments. It was used to establish a profile of the Canadian academic economics profession, with reference to its connections with other countries. (A second, smaller questionnaire, was used only for its income information in the original, larger manuscript).

(5) *The Commonwealth Universities Yearbook, 1965*, university calendars, and correspondence with Professor M. Von Zur-Muehlen were helpful in interpreting the sample.

schooling took place. Readers who avoid our footnotes describing the calculations should, however, note the following special decisions, differing a little from the earlier chapter.[6]

[6]Mimeographed copies of the original study, of which this chapter forms a part, are available from A. D. Scott, Economics Department, University of British Columbia, Vancouver, Canada.

1. Having information on the stocks of foreign-born in both the Canadian and American professions makes it possible to look at the gains and losses from both points of view. In the earlier students' calculation, on the other hand, we had information only on the stock and flow of foreign students within the United States.

2. *Opportunity cost*. There are two competing assumptions about the burden of opportunity cost of study while in a foreign country: that it is borne by the home country (the student might have been working at home instead of studying abroad), or is borne in the country of study (the immigrant student might have worked instead of studying). We investigated the sensitivity of our balance-sheet to these assumptions, in view of the fact that the recent estimate by Parai on Canadian students abroad assumed that the opportunity cost is borne by Canada.

3. *Self-Support*. Our original estimate is based upon the assumption that a very small proportion of Canadian graduate students in the U.S. are supported by any but U.S. sources; for the sake of clarity, we put this proportion at zero. However, it is possible that Canadian students carry with them considerable Canadian funds in the form of scholarships, earnings from past summer work, parental allowances, and so forth. We do not know. To bring out the effect of our assumption, we offer an alternative balance sheet in which the proportion of self-support is put at 50 per cent.

The Balance Sheets. We now proceed to calculate our "original" balance, as shown in Tables 11.1 and 11.2. Each table is worked out in Canadian values and prices and the totals only are also given in American values (explained below).

Column 1 shows the numbers of students who have attained each kind of degree (for example, 88 persons now in the U.S. attended elementary school in Canada). Column 2 shows our estimate of the 1964 resource cost of this education per student. Column 3 shows the opportunity cost of this education, per student. Columns 4, 5, and 6 then show the total of these costs for all the degrees shown in column 1.

It can be seen that the largest total magnitudes stem from the costs of education in high school and university, the large number of years in elementary school being more than offset by the small unit costs of such education and the absence of opportunity costs at these ages.

The last line of Table 11.2 gives totals in American values, which differ from Canadian values for the following main reasons: opportunity costs of higher education in the U.S. are estimated to be considerably higher than in Canada; and, second, the educational cost of graduate studies has been estimated to be far larger in Canada than in the United States. The first point is easily deduced from inspection of wage-rate statistics in the two countries. The second, though surprising, is confirmed by independent studies by Parai and Wilkinson.[7]

[7] For example, a year of M.A. work is costed at $4,143 in Canada, but only at $2,437 in the U.S. This arises from assuming that, in Canada as in the U.S., graduate costs are four times

Table 11.1

Canadian Contribution to the Stock of Economists in the U.S. in 1964

		Average cost per student		Total cost—all students		
Type of education	(1) Number of degrees	(2) Education cost	(3) Opportunity cost	(4) (1)x(2)	(5) (1)x(3)	(6) (4)+(5)
Elementary	88	260 x 8 yrs	—	183,040	—	183,040
High School	88	538 x 4 yrs	915 x 4	189,376	322,080	511,456
B.A.	44	1,377 x 4 yrs	1,800 x 4	242,352	316,800	559,152
M.A.	26	4,143 x 2 yrs	1,800 x 2	215,436	93,600	309,036
Ph.D.	7	4,143 x 2 yrs	1,800 x 2	58,002	25,200	83,202
Total in Canadian Values				888,206	757,680	1,645,886
Total in American Values				784,586	994,708	1,779,294

Sources and Methods: Column 1: The numbers of Canadian degrees are taken from the NSF-AEA survey cards. Of the 12 individuals who left Canada before completing high school (as shown in the survey returns), it was assumed that 6 attended elementary school in Canada. Of the 88 persons who attended high school in Canada, 77 were Canadian-born and 11 were U.S.-born. Of this latter group we assumed five took their elementary education in Canada and six did not. This gives 77 + 6 + 5 = 88 for elementary schooling in Canada.

Row 1, col. 2: From Wilkinson, Table III-10 and Appendix III Table A, 115 and 263-4. The consumer price index was used to carry Wilkinson's $253 to 1963-4 levels.

Row 1, col. 3: Chapter 10 and Schultz, "Education and Economic Growth," in Nelson B. Henry, ed., *Social Forces Influencing American Education* (Chicago, 1961).

Row 2, col. 2: Wilkinson, as for Row 1 col. 2. This figure includes institutional costs but excludes incidentals such as books, supplies, and transportation, which we have deducted from Wilkinson (and Schultz).

Row 2, col. 3: Source: Wilkinson, Table III-10, gives $855 as the annual opportunity costs of a high school student in Canada in 1961-2. Wilkinson depends on Schultz's U.S. figure and the Canadian census data on high school and university earnings. These seem a little high, as there is no adjustment for unemployment in 1961-2. In moving the estimate to 1963-4, therefore, it is raised by 7 per cent rather than the 11 per cent indicated in the DBS manufacturing earnings index.

Row 3, col. 2: Source: *Canadian Universities, Income and Expenditure, 1963-4*, DBS No. 81-212, Table 10 and p. 34. The distinction between education and research, extension, etc., costs made in Chapter 10 is maintained here. Basing ourselves on the percentage allocation of expenditure shown by DBS, we estimate that of the $289 million total expenditure, 61.2 per cent was direct instructional and departmental research, and of the remaining 38.8 per cent overhead, only 25 percentage points may be allocated to instruction and departmental research. (This corresponds almost exactly with the finding in Chapter 10 for the U.S., that one-third of overhead applies to organized research and external activities, and should be disregarded.) The total, therefore, is (61.2 + 25 per cent) of $289 = $249 millions.

The overhead cost was allocated equally to graduates and undergraduates. Instructional and departmental research costs were estimated to be 4 times greater for graduates than for undergraduates (Chapter 10). This yields $1,377 for undergraduates and $4,143 for graduates. Wilkinson, p. 70 gives figures rather higher than this, chiefly because he did not reduce overhead for organized research, etc., partly because he seems to have allowed for depreciation and interest on total plant in an arbitrary way instead of using reported figures, and partly because he makes no distinction between graduate and undergraduate costs. The Canadian $1,377, obtained in this way, is surprisingly higher than our $1,023 for a U.S. undergraduate year.

Row 3, col. 3: See row 2 col. 3, above. Source here is G. Rosenbluth, *CAUT Bulletin* (December 1965, February 1966), 25, who shows earnings foregone as $2,500 and summer earnings as $710, yielding our $1,800. Rosenbluth uses data from DBS No. 81-520, and is rather lower than Wilkinson, who bases himself on the 1961 census.

Row 4, col. 3 and row 5 col. 3: Opportunity costs taken to be same as for B.A. students. Both the lowness of opportunity costs, and the attribution of the same opportunity costs to different levels of education, are arguable but customary inputs in our, and other studies.

Row 7: American totals calculated using: Schultz, "Education and Economic Growth"; T. W. Schultz, "Capital Formation by Education," *Journal of Political Economy* 68 (December 1960):571-83; Grubel and Scott, "U.S. College Student Exchange."

Table 11.2

American Contribution to the Stock of Academic Economists in Canada in 1964

Type of education	(1) Number of degrees	Average cost per student (2) Education cost	(3) Opportunity cost	Total cost—all students (4) (1) x (2)	(5) (1) x (3)	(6) (4) x (5)
Elementary	34 (19 x 1.8)	260 x 8 yrs	—	70,720	—	70,720
High School	31 (17 x 1.8)	538 x 4 yrs	915 x 4	66,712	113,460	180,172
Bachelor of Arts	43 (24 x 1.8)	1,377 x 4 yrs	1,800 x 4	236,844	309,600	546,444
Master of Arts	106 (76 x 1.4)	4,143 x 2 yrs	1,800 x 2	878,316	381,600	1,259,916
Doctor of Philosophy	125 (125 x 1)	4,143 x 2 yrs	1,800 x 2	1,035,750	450,000	1,485,750
Total in Canadian Values				2,288,342	1,254,660	3,543,002
Total in American Values				1,553,486	1,725,576	3,279,062

Sources: Column 1: These multipliers were obtained from consideration of the following information: (a) the count of U.S. Ph.D.'s is believed to be complete; (b) the total sample is believed to be about 1.00/1.75 of the number of academic economists; (c) the sample is most deficient among colleges with proportionately few Ph.D.'s. Consequently, the multipliers were set at 1.0 for Ph.D.'s and 1.8 for B.A.'s and 1.4 obtained for M.A.'s by interpolation.

We may now confront Tables 11.1 and 11.2. The first shows holders of Canadian degrees now in the U.S., and the second shows holders of American degrees now in Canada. (Thus, while there are only 7 Ph.D.'s granted by Canada in the U.S., there are 125 Ph.D.'s granted by U.S. institutions now in Canada.) The balance is struck in Table 11.3. Based on the totals in Tables 11.1 and 11.2, it shows that, using Canadian values, the "net gain to Canada" was about $1,900,000; in U.S. values, the "net loss to the U.S." was about $1,500,000.

Table 11.3

"Net Gain" to Canada and "Net Loss" to U.S. from International Movements of Economists Using Opportunity Costs of Canadian Economists with American Training

U.S. contribution to training Canadian economists (Table 11.2)	$3,543,002
Canadian contribution to training American economists (Table 11.1)	$1,645,886
Balance: "net gain to Canada" (in Canadian values)	$1,897,116
Balance: "net loss to U.S." (in American values)	$1,499,768

In Table 11.4, we examine the costs of training the economists in Canada at the stages enumerated in Table 11.2 by dividing these economists into Canadian-born, foreign- (non-U.S.) born, and U.S.-born. The purpose of this subdivision of the earlier total gross Canadian gain from U.S. contribution to training Canadian economists is to show how much of the gain is simple U.S. input into the total education of Americans who then move to Canada (migration). The residue, foreign-born Canadian economists trained in the U.S., is a mixed bag containing not only American citizens born outside the U.S., but also foreigners who were only in the U.S. long enough to acquire a degree.

From the table it can be seen that the gross Canadian gain (in Canadian funds and prices) of $3.543 million is built up as follows: 54 per cent the education of Canadian-born; 30 per cent the education of U.S.-born; and 16 per cent the education of foreign-born. Thus, the answer to the question posed in the first paragraph is that the U.S. contribution to the "reflux" was approximately double (54/30) the U.S. contribution embodied in American

undergraduate costs. Thus, the $1,500 difference between the two countries is four times the difference between the undergraduate costs, for which see Wilkinson, *Studies in the Economics of Education*, Appendix 2. We have no independent check on this four-fold ratio, but have checked that a more moderate multiplier for Canada would not change the final balance between the two countries: the Canadian favorable balance exists at U.S. values.

Table 11.4

American Contribution to the Stock of Academic Economists in Canada, 1964, by Country of Birth

Type of education	Canadian-born economists with American degrees in Canada in 1964	Foreign-born economists with American degrees in Canada in 1964	American-born economists with American degrees in Canada in 1964	Average cost per student		U.S. contribution			
				Education cost	Opportunity cost	Total cost Canadian-born	Total cost foreign-born	Total cost American-born	Total Canadian gain
	(1)	(2)	(3)	(4)	(5)	(6)	(7)	(8)	(9)
Elementary	0	0	34	260 x 8	—	—	—	70,720	70,720
High School	2	0	29	538 x 4	914 x 4	11,624	—	168,548	180,172
Bachelor of Arts	9	5	29	1,337 x 4	1,800 x 4	114,372	63,540	368,532	546,444
Master of Arts	69	18	20	4,143 x 2	1,800 x 2	820,134	213,948	237,720	1,271,802
Doctor of Philosophy	80	24	20	4,143 x 2	1,800 x 2	950,880	285,264	237,720	1,473,864
Total in Canadian Values						1,897,010	562,752	1,083,240	3,543,002
Per Cent in Canadian Values						54%	16%	30%	100%
Total in American Values						1,673,210	502,592	1,103,260	3,279,062
Per Cent in American Values						51%	15%	34%	100%

Notes: Columns 1, 2, 3: sample questionnaire results multiplied by the appropriate multiplier. (See notes to Figure 11.1 and Table 11.2.)

migration to Canada. And of the overwhelming 54 per cent, the largest single part (27 percentage points) is the education of Canadian-born Ph.D.'s who subsequently returned to Canada. This is most clearly seen in column 6, line 5, of Table 11.4. It amounts to $950,880, a very large amount indeed. The composition of the American "gross loss," worked out in U.S. values, is approximately the same, a slightly higher percentage being attributed to the education of U.S.-born. This is because it is only among the American-born that dearer education and opportunity costs of elementary and high school show up; Canadian-born and foreign-born economists did not go to American public schools.

ALTERNATIVE TREATMENTS OF OPPORTUNITY COST

The preceding paragraphs and tables have been based on the premise that total cost of education is the sum of the resource cost of training and the opportunity cost of using time for study rather than for production. This familiar approach to human-capital studies, applied to international movements, implies a theory that the burden of opportunity cost falls on the host country—the country where the education is taking place. But this theory can only be justified by this point of view: that the major choice open to the persons whose mobility is studied is not "In which country shall I study?" but "Being in this country, shall I study or shall I work?" Because these persons' migration is taken for granted, but their studying is not, the decision to study is consequently viewed as imposing an opportunity cost upon the host country.

When we examine the careers of the people on whom we have data, we see that there is one group at least for whom that point of view is quite inappropriate: students who go abroad to study, and then return to their own country. It is clear from their careers that the purpose of migrating was study, and that if they had decided to work instead they would have remained at home to do so. Consequently, for this group at least we must remove the host country cost of foregone earnings and substitute for it the cost of maintenance.[8]

Fortunately for brevity, this substitution will not require a wholesale reworking of our estimates. For it does not need to be applied to Canadians going to the U.S. and staying there, nor to Americans or foreigners coming to Canada to work as economists. For them the "gain" to their new country (or "loss" to their former country) is the earnings foregone while they were

[8]This substitution makes the treatment of foreign students here similar to that in Chapter 10. An alternative would be to attribute the opportunity costs of foreign study to the home country rather than to the host; this is the procedure used by Parai, *Immigration and Emigration . . .*, p. 122, for a rather different purpose. Wilkinson, *Studies in the Economics of Education*, pp. 70-79, does not consider returning students. We should record a useful suggestion by a reader for the *Canadian Journal of Economics* that, instead of a two-way balance of indebtedness, a study might well utilize a three-way attribution of costs: to the migrant; to all other Canadians; and to all other Americans.

students, as shown in the estimates already explained. It need be applied only to two groups: Americans studying in Canada then returning to the U.S.; and Canadians studying in the U.S. and then returning to Canada. The former group was so small as to be considered zero, and hence, may be neglected. The latter group, however, is large.

The reworking necessitated is shown in Table 11.5. We have substituted for opportunity cost the maintenance costs shown in column 3. These are set at $1,700 in Canada and $2,385 in the United States. (The discrepancy is larger than we would have expected, but is based on evidence from two sources.) Neither figure includes international transportation, but only "domestic transport," which is thought to be large enough to cover most Canadian-American movements.

How much difference does this substitution make to the "net gains" calculated in the previous section? The new balance, adjusted for maintenance costs shows that the difference is negligible: in Canadian terms, for example, Canada still "gains" $1,856,396 (shown at the bottom of the left half of the table).

Self-Support. So far, we have assumed that students going abroad to study are entirely the guests of their host country. Our discussion of the U.S. foreign-student exchange, however, will have made clear that a final adjustment is necessary to our balance: we must allow for the fact that students going abroad do not all (or entirely) depend on the generosity of the host country, but to varying degrees "support themselves" while abroad. In our calculations, this adjustment must be made to the education costs imposed by two groups: Americans who have been trained in Canada, and Canadians who have been trained in the United States. (For lack of information, we neglect foreigners who trained in one of the countries then migrated to the other. We believe that their careers would change the gross totals, but not the net balance between Canada and the United States.)

The group of Americans who have been trained in Canada is so small as to be safely neglected. The group of Canadians trained in the United States must now be further subdivided into two groups: not only those who have studied in the U.S. and returned to Canada (who were dealt with in the previous section on maintenance costs), but also a new group, those who on completing their studies in the U.S., remained there. The greater the "self-support" of these two subgroups, the smaller the net U.S. contribution in the final balance.

As discussed already, in Chapter 10, self-support can be visualized as an amalgam of three kinds of student financing: Canadians carrying Canadian scholarships and other transfers from Canadian sources; Canadians carrying their own Canadian earnings for spending in the U.S.; and Canadians earning funds from interrupting their studies to work while in the U.S. We have reason to believe that all three sources are important. A little application of balance-of-payments theory shows that it does not matter whether the funds are carried from Canada or earned by Canadians in the U.S.: in either case they reduce the net "gain" of Canada by the amount that Canada has in effect "remitted" to the U.S.

How great is the magnitude of this self-support? We do not know, but we do know that not only do Canadian students frequently carry grants and past earnings but also frequently depend on work as teaching assistants, research assistants, and so forth as ways of supporting themselves. Frequently regarded as "scholarships" from U.S. sources, the latter are actually forms of self-support. Having no information on the magnitude of self-support, we have made what we regard as an extreme assumption: that one-half of tuition fees and one-half of maintenance costs are paid by self-support. We now investigate the effect of this extreme assumption on our previous net balance.

The adjustments, though laborious, are in principle simple. In Table 11.5, columns 5-9, we take the data of columns 1-4 dealing with Canadians studying in the U.S. and returning to Canada. Because we now assume 50 per cent self-support, one-half the tuition fees are subtracted from education cost (leaving not only the other half but the rest of education cost not covered by fees); and one-half of maintenance cost is deducted. In Canadian terms, this reduces the gross U.S. contribution of $1,856,290 (column 4) to $1,290,521 (column 9).

For reasons already explained, we leave the education and opportunity costs of foreigners unchanged.

In Table 11.5 (columns 10-13) we turn to a set of costs that have not so far entered our balance: the education costs, *in the* U.S. of Canadians who, after graduate training did not return to Canada. These have so far been regarded as U.S. costs of increasing the U.S. stock of human capital and so irrelevant to our calculations. However, it is just as reasonable to argue that these students were self-supported to the same extent as those who were subsequently attracted back to Canada. Consequently, "remittances" to them are part of the Canadian contribution to the U.S. stock, or an offset to the U.S. contribution to Canada.

Table 11.1 shows the distribution of Canadian degrees among the U.S. stock of Canadians. Table 11.5 (columns 10-13) shows the total cost of their subsequent education in the U.S., and the Canadian contribution to their tuition fees and maintenance.[9]

SUMMARY

Our final net balance, in Canadian and U.S. values is shown at the bottom of Table 11.5. It is shown that our extreme assumption, that one-half tuition fees and maintenance of Canadian students abroad was paid as "remittances" from Canada, reduces the net U.S. contribution of $1,856,396 to

[9]We have had to make reasonable guesses at the distribution of further education among the Canadians.

Table 11.5

Maintenance Cost and Self-Support in the American Contribution to the Stock of Canadian Academic Economists, 1964

Type of education	Cdn.-born econ. with U.S. deg. in Can. in 1964	Average cost per student		U.S. contribution (total cost) Cdn.-born using maint. cost (1)[(2) + (3)]	Equiv. Cdn.-born econ. with U.S. deg. in Can. in 1964 (50%) Cdn. self-support (1) x 1/2	Self-support in U.S. values			Net U.S. cont. [(4)-(8)]	Cdn. contribution to train U.S. econ. before adding for self-support (Table 11.1)	Self-supported students remain in U.S.		Cdn. Contribution including self-support (10) + (12)
		Educ. cost	Maint. cost			Tuition cost	Maint. cost	Total			No. of deg.	Total self-support [11(6x7)] x1.08	
	(1)	(2)	(3)	(4)	(5)	(6)	(7)	(8)	(9)	(10)	(11)	(12)	(13)
Elem.	0	—	—	—	0	—	—	0	—	183,040	—	—	183,040
H.S.	2	538x4	—	4,304	1	—	—	0	4,304	511,456	—	—	511,456
B.A.	9	1,337x4	1,700x4	110,772	5	378x4	2,385x4	59,681	51,091	559,152	22	262,595	821,747
M.A.	69	4,143x2	1,700x2	806,334	35	739x2	2,385x2	237,164	570,160	309,036	29	195,687	504,723
Ph.D.	80	4,143x2	1,700x2	934,880	40	739x2	2,385x2	269,914	664,966	83,202	30	202,435	285,637
Total				1,856,290				565,769	1,290,521	1,645,886		660,717	2,306,603

"Net Gain" to Canada in Canadian values using Maintenance Cost [Table 11.4: (7) + (8)] + [Table 11.5: (4)] - [Table 11.1: (6)] $3,502,282 - $1,645,886 = $1,856,396
"Net Loss" to U.S. in U.S. values using maintenance cost = $1,450,530.

"Net Gain" to Canada in Canadian values taking into account self-support. [Table 11.4: (7) + (8)] + [Table 11.5: (9)] - [Table 11.5: (10) + (12)] $2,936,513 - $2,306,603 = $629,910
"Net Loss" to U.S. in U.S. values taking into account self-support = $224,044.

Notes: Column 3: Canadian maintenance costs.

1. Rosenbluth, *CAUT Bulletin* (Feb. 1966), 25. Living costs are $1,030. Incidental expenses are $200.
2. Canada, *DBS Bulletin*, 81-520, "University Student Expenditure and Income in Canada 1961/62," Part II, 38. Figures for a single student living away from home, 1963/64 cost assumed the same as in 1961/62.
3. R. Rabinovitch, *An Analysis of the Canadian Post Secondary Student Population* (Ottawa, 1966), 66 and 85.
4. Since the *DBS* figures ($1,030 + $200) do not include transportation costs for out-of-town students and are based on only an eight month period we have made the following adjustments: (i) added $100 for transportation; (ii) added $400 to adjust for 12 months to arrive at the $1,700 figure used in column 3.

Column 6: Average tuition fees times number of years. Because self-supported students paid U.S. fees, these are American fees. As in Chapter 10, Table 11.5, lines 16 and 17, graduate fees are assumed to be 28 per cent, and undergraduate fees 37 per cent of their direct education costs. (For graduates, this percentage was also reached by a detailed examination of fees at schools apparently attended by Canadian-born economists; for undergraduates the 37 per cent is probably low, neglecting the fact that many Canadians would pay out-of-state fees.)

Column 7: Maintenance costs from Chapter 10.

Column 8: Col. 5 x (col. 6 + col. 7), all multiplied by 1.08, the U.S.-Canada exchange rate at the time.

Column 9: Col. 4-col. 8.

Column 10: from Table 11.1.

Column 11: In order to find the value of self-support in tuition and maintenance it was necessary to discover the number of U.S. degrees, the costs of which might have been "self-supported," held by Canadians now in the U.S. The NSF-AEA cards give some, but not all such degrees. The assumed careers are shown in the following chart, yielding 44 U.S. B.A.'s; 58 U.S. M.A.'s; and 59 U.S. Ph.D.'s. Half these numbers are written into column 11. The reconstruction of these careers is based partly on the numbers of which these degrees are their holders' highest degrees, and partly on the distribution of careers of similar economists who returned to Canada.

	UNITED STATES Number of degrees	UNITED STATES number of highest degrees	CANADA degree
Born		1 (1)	89 (88)
High School		(44)	88 (44)
BA	44 (2) (42)	4 (2) (16)	44 (26)
MA	58 (12) (46)	13 (6) (13)	26 (7)
Ph.D	59 (59)	66 (7)	7
TOTAL	——	89	——

Column 12: Col. 11 x (col. 6 + col. 7) all multiplied by 1.08, the U.S.-Canada exchange rate at the time.
Column 13: Col. 10 + Col. 12.

$629,910 in Canadian terms. Readers who believe our 50 per cent guess is too extreme may substitute their own compromise. Almost any reasonable figure will lead to the same final conclusion, that in spite of the fact that there are 89 "Canadian economists" in the Canadian stock, Canada is nevertheless "indebted" to the United States for between one-half and one-million dollars in the net international exchange of persons and training.

This, we believe, is a striking refutation of the frequently heard suggestion that a large stock of one's nationals abroad indicates a large brain drain. Our human-capital approach, evaluating Canadian inputs into the U.S. stock and U.S. inputs into the Canadian stock, has shown that a mere counting of heads leads to the wrong conclusion.

We would suggest that the application of this kind of study to other professions and skills would be a valuable corrective to the generally accepted brain drain myth. While it is true that because of their mobility Canadian economists are not typical of other Canadian professions (as was admitted earlier), it is clear that even the sign of the net balance of any profession's brain drain cannot be guessed at without such calculations as these.[10]

Does this net balance of "indebtedness" indicate who has gained or lost in the international flows? If education, maintenance and opportunity costs measured human capital prospectively as well as retrospectively, the answer must be yes. But what if the economic students who have eventually settled in the United States are, or embody, human capital superior to that of the economists who have returned to Canada? (Harry Johnson[11] and Mabel Timlin[12] can be interpreted as believing this to be the fact.) Our earlier study on the United States economic profession casts some doubt on this, however, by finding no evidence in income or employment that as a

[10]Furthermore, it appears that our calculations tend to throw some shadow of doubt on the ingenious flow calculations of Professor Wilkinson, which he uses to measure the human capital embodied in all Canadian immigrants and emigrants during the years 1951-61, and which he concludes with the perfectly proper comment: "It should be evident from the above study that it is important to look beyond the absolute numbers of persons involved in international migration and consider the dollar values of the human capital flows as well. Only in this way could we hope to arrive at any realistic assessment of the dollar gains and losses involved" (p. 79). However, he unfortunately illustrates this conclusion by showing that while emigration, in absolute numbers, amounts to only about 20 per cent of immigration, the superior human capital embodied in Canadian emigrants raises the "loss" by Canada to about 30 per cent of the value of immigrants. If Professor Wilkinson had considered also the contribution of other countries to the education of Canadians, the cost of emigration would have been reduced again, toward his original 20 per cent level. It does appear too that our technique of considering stocks may be more fruitful than his technique of considering flows in obtaining information on the characteristics of migrants.

[11]H. G. Johnson, "Canadian Contributions to the Discipline of Economics Since 1945," *Canadian Journal of Economics*, 1, 1 (February 1968): 129-146.

[12]Mabel Timlin, "Social Research in Canada," in A. Faucher and M. Timlin, *Social Sciences in Canada* (Ottawa, 1968).

group foreign economists in the U.S. are superior to native-born.[13] This confirms that economists migrate because they increase their own capital value, not because they are better than those whom they leave, or those they join. And if Canadian migrants are not superior to U.S. economists, why should they be assumed to be superior to Canadian economists? More research is needed, but it is so far entirely possible that the U.S. "indebtedness" measured in terms of future productivity will be of the same sign as that measured by past costs.[14]

[13]Grubel and Scott, "Foreigners in the U.S. Economics Profession."

[14]Whether "foreign training" means anything to the quality of a country's professionals is a familiar question in other contexts. See Robert I. Crane, "Technical Education and Economic Development in India before World War I," in C. A. Anderson and M. J. Bowman, *Education and Economic Development* (Chicago: University of Chicago Press, 1967), pp. 167-201; and C. V. Kidd, "The Economics of the Brain Drain," *Minerva*, 4, 1 (Autumn 1965): 105-107, for discussion of the importance of domestic training for domestic specialists. Recent surveys in Canada by K. W. Taylor, "Economic Scholarship in Canada," *Canadian Journal of Economics and Political Science*, 26, 1 (February 1960): 6-18; J. H. Dales, "Canadian Scholarship in Economics: Achievement and Outlook," an address to the Royal Society of Canada, 7 June 1967; Scott, "Recruitment and Migration"; H. G. Johnson, "The Social Sciences in the Age of Opulence," *Canadian Journal of Economics and Political Science*, 32, 4 (November 1966): 423-442; D. Smiley, "Contributions to Canadian Political Science since the Second World War," *Canadian Journal of Economics and Political Science*, 33, 4 (November 1967): 569-580; R. A. Preston, "Two-Way Traffic in Canadian History," *Queen's Quarterly* 74 (Autumn 1967): 380-391. All touch on the effect of foreign standards, training or scholarship on the quality of Canadian academic disciplines.

Part III

POLICY STUDY

Chapter 12

POLICIES TO REDUCE OR MODIFY THE BRAIN DRAIN

The preceding chapters of this book contain both analysis and statistics helpful in arriving at an informed view of the impact of the international migration of highly-skilled persons. The material cannot be summarized easily and there are many loose ends in the statistics and arguments. However, a careful study of the available evidence permits everyone to make some personal guess as to the loss of welfare the brain drain in recent years has brought to the world.

Such a guess is a necessary part of judging the acceptability of specific recommendations designed to reduce or modify the brain drain. Each of these recommendations can be implemented only at a certain social cost and acceptability depends on whether the benefits from the reduced brain drain exceed the costs incurred in the implementation of the policy. The remaining part of this chapter discusses individual policies from this point of view.

Specific recommendations for policies to reduce the brain drain are implicitly or explicitly based on the recognition of three important causes of the migration: the search for higher money income, for greater professional opportunities and for greater personal freedom. These three motives are highly correlated in the sense that personal freedom is a necessary though not sufficient condition for adequate professional opportunities which in turn often lead to higher incomes. Furthermore, in countries where income levels are low, professional opportunities also tend to be scarce and political instability and lack of personal freedom are frequent. However, it is analytically convenient and according to the research of psychologists[1] empirically meaningful to distinguish between those incentives for migration working only on money income and those working through psychological income, especially satisfaction with professional activities.

NARROWING THE INCOME GAP

Policies to stop the brain drain can readily be classified into four major groups. The first of these sees the solution in a reduction of the income differences throughout the world. The attainment of this objective has been and will continue to be one of the prime concerns of men interested in

[1] James A. Wilson, "The Emigration of British Scientists," *Minerva* 5, 1 (Autumn 1966): 20-29; and Herbert G. Grubel and Anthony D. Scott, "Determinants of Migration: The Highly Skilled," *International Migration*, 5, 2 (1967), Chapters 2 and 6.

building a better world for all mankind. The fact that the equalization of world incomes may reduce the net flow of highly skilled persons between countries is of trivial importance in relation to the other gains for the welfare of the world flowing from the attainment of this objective and it probably adds no significant incentive to the efforts for economic development in the low income countries of the world. As Dr. Charles Kidd has said: "Economic and social development as a positive goal is much more significant than reducing or stopping the brain drain as a negative goal."[2]

The narrowing of income differences rather than their elimination may well reduce the brain drain significantly because potential migrants' ties to their families, friends and culture and the psychological and monetary cost of moving are barriers to mobility which only relatively high income differences tend to overcome. In this sense, programs for narrowing worldwide income differences hold for a solution of the brain drain problem well before incomes are equalized. However, economic development may also increase incentives for migration and the brain drain. Larger stocks of highly skilled persons and centers of research and learning tend to become targets for increased hiring by the more developed countries. Western Europe's flow of highly skilled manpower to the United States and Canada indicated that relatively high levels of economic development will not prevent the brain drain. For these reasons, economic development is, at best, only a long run solution to the basic problem. On the other hand, it may be possible to use incomes to retain "key" scientific personnel. Because scientists do not migrate for income alone, but also for scientific opportunity, it is likely that some of them would be less inclined to emigrate if their seniors were committed by *their* incomes to remaining. By keeping the coach and captains, the rest of the team may hold together. Universities can confirm this policy, in that financial decline has affected staff quality only after a long lag during which time committed seniors have attracted dedicated juniors.

NARROWING THE OPPORTUNITY GAP

The second group of policy recommendations is concerned with equalizing opportunities for personal and professional development of highly skilled persons throughout the world.

One set of policies in this group can be categorized as avoiding conditions of excess demand and supply through better planning for highly educated manpower in both the developed and developing countries.

[2]Prepared statement by Charles Kidd, "The Brain Drain of Scientists, Engineers and Physicians from the Developing Countries to the United States," in *The Brain Drain into the United States of Scientists, Engineers, and Physicians* Hearings, U.S. Congress, House of Representatives, Committee on Government Operations, 90th Congress, 1st session, 1967, p. 47.

In the developing countries two separate causes for a current and prospective excess supply of highly skilled persons can be identified. In democracies, such as India, expenditure on education and the number of university graduates are politically determined. As a result of upper-middle class demand for higher education, which since colonial times had been the route to highly paid civil service jobs of superior status, the number of university graduates has been increased rapidly and the average quality of their skills has declined. India has now a substantial excess supply of university graduates holding degrees which are not greatly valued as a qualification for productive employment.

In some African countries the problem of excess supply has not yet arisen but may appear soon as a result of a process in which the rate of output of highly educated persons has been fixed to meet the demand arising from the replacement of European colonial administrators and from the anticipated growth in the economy. Once the replacement demand has been met, the existing rate of supply will be too large to meet the specialized demand stemming from economic growth alone. Aggravating this situation is the existing salary structure, which like India's is a remnant from colonial times when highly skilled persons from Western Europe had to be attracted by relatively high salaries. These high salaries now represent strong incentives for young men to enter administrative professions, and as a result supply threatens to exceed the governments' ability to hire persons at these levels of remuneration. Such private industry as exists is unable to attract these men because at salaries competitive with those paid by the government, their productivity is below their pay.[3]

The public demand for higher education in many less-developed countries has found a positive response in governmental circles because of the notion, which had almost become an intellectual fad during the last decade, that "the road to economic development is paved with universities."[4] In recent years a reaction has set in against this unrealistic appraisal of the economic development process. In the meantime, however, many countries have produced excessive numbers of graduates, some highly skilled, who, because of their lack of professional opportunities at home are seeking employment abroad. The avoidance of such future excess supply conditions in the less-developed countries will lead to a reduction in the brain drain.

In the United States highly skilled persons are attracted from abroad as a result of conditions of excess demand. Thus, practices by the American

[3]Statement by Adams, *The Brain Drain*, p. 55. In India, however, there is now some complaint that the over-supply has led to the picking off of the best qualified graduates by foreign-owned firms. This complaint suggests that government salaries are no longer higher than industry's.

[4]Charles A. Myers, "The Importance of Higher Education to Development," in *Higher Education and the International Flow of Manpower: Implications for the Developing World* (University of Minnesota, 1967).

Medical Association restricting the supply of doctors in conjunction with massive government medical care and health research programs have created an excess demand for medical personnel. The sudden increase in government research and development efforts in space projects similarly has created opportunities for the employment of foreign scientists and technologists. In the United Kingdom it was decided that the government cost of free medical care would be held down by increasing the supply of physicians through educational subsidies and by keeping down salaries paid to them during their working lives. From the standpoint of economic theory this policy should, in a closed economy, produce as many physicians as does one in which education is not subsidized but the doctors' investment in their skills is repaid through higher earnings as practitioners. However, the first policy is distinctly inferior to the second in an open economy where physicians are free to leave with their subsidized education and earn high incomes in another country. Better planning of government projects with special concern for the effects on available manpower, together with the elimination of private barriers to entry, would reduce conditions of excess demand and supply and thereby diminish the resultant brain drain.[5]

One important aspect of unrealistic manpower planning has to do with the non-return of students sent abroad to complete their education. The fault lies, on the part of the less-developed countries, in their failure to select with the proper care students wishing to acquire skills necessary or at least integratable into a general development plan, so that they can be assured of positions upon their return home. There should be a greater concentration of resources on foreign studies in professional skills not taught in the native country and a relative decrease in the number of students seeking general education at the undergraduate level. (In general, countries should be encouraged to set manpower programs or forecasts that allow for or predict the loss of certain percentage of their students abroad through non-return, thus avoiding critical manpower shortages.) In the developed countries efforts should be made to provide courses of study for foreign students which will meet the demands of their native countries, and thus increase their opportunities for adequate employment upon their return. Foreign students should be discouraged from, and not rewarded for, working on highly sophisticated research projects which tend to over-educate them for the tasks facing them on their return home.

All of the preceding arguments and policy recommendations are based on the premise that "manpower forecasting" *can* provide the necessary information for the avoidance of conditions of excess demand and supply.

[5]This interpretation of the situation facing the British medical profession, suggested to us by Professor Harry G. Johnson, does, however, tend to ignore the burden of foregone earnings during five to seven years of training, and to over-emphasize the attractive power of low fees and board. See Chapter 6.

However, recent experience has shown that the technique of predicting and programming that is usually termed "manpower planning" is poorly developed and has had a rather dismal record. In its present state, it can at best provide broad perspectives, the most important of which is to set educational systems so that they provide the greatest possible number of professional alternatives to the highly educated as late in their training as possible, thus enabling the supply of skills to respond quickly to unforeseen changes in demand.[6] Perhaps manpower prediction can in the long run provide better information and avoid the appearance of international differences in professional opportunities through the existence of excess demand and supply. In the near future, however, there is little hope for the relief of the brain drain problem through better manpower planning. Mistakes will continue to be made, especially as the rate of technological change increases, and to the extent that they occur the brain drain is not a scourge but a blessing in that it permits individuals and the world to minimize the consequences of having made expensive, wrong investments in skills.

Proposals have been made to dictate precise courses of study to foreign students in order to avoid that they be "spoiled" for the type of tasks awaiting them in their native countries. Thus, students are to be restricted especially from working on technically highly sophisticated research projects. However, such restrictions tend to limit the quality and quantity of education available to them. In some fields of science, such as chemistry and physics, it is difficult to find a senior professor to sponsor a thesis unless the student is willing and able to be part of the professor's major research effort. Moreover, such restrictions result in a loss to the world of the truly exceptional research talent which is likely to be found among students from abroad. These disadvantages must be weighed carefully in discussions about policies to stem the brain drain through restrictions of the freedom of foreign students to choose their own fields of study and to determine the length of time they will devote to them.

In the class of policies aimed at equalizing professional opportunities throughout the world and thus reduce incentives for the brain drain is contained an additional set of those which are designed to increase the job satisfaction of those highly skilled persons already at work. Of greatest long-term importance would be a movement towards the recognition of achievement in countries where status at birth, family and caste relationships determine social and occupational opportunities. The isolation of scientists in many less-developed countries from the world centers of learning can be relieved by the establishment of institutes where scientists from all parts of the world hold temporary positions[7] and by more bilateral

[6]Mark Blaug, "Approaches to Educational Planning," *Economic Journal*, 77, 306 (June 1967).

[7]Abdus Salam, "The Isolation of the Scientist in Developing Countries," *Minerva* 4, 4 (Summer 1966): 461-465.

exchanges of teachers and research workers between universities in developed and developing countries. The near free distribution of scientific publications to interested institutions in less-developed countries would afford scientists there the opportunity to keep up with recent developments in their field and reduce their feeling of isolation. Such contacts among the world's scientists and the free distribution of knowledge can be expected to have a high rate of return, since the marginal social costs of such exchange programs and of producing extra copies of print are very low and the long-term benefits to scientific progress, as well as the reduction of the brain drain, can be expected to be very large.[8]

In general, all of these recommendations for the improvement of professional opportunities and accomplishment in less-developed countries aimed at reducing the brain drain have far-reaching positive effects on worldwide scientific progress and the quality of life in these countries, which are probably at least as important as the effects on the brain drain. However, as with the policies directed at narrowing the income differences, they can be expected to become effective only over a long period. Nevertheless, the existence of the brain drain gives still greater urgency to the vigorous pursuit of these policies.

MAKING MIGRATION MORE DIFFICULT

The third major group of policies is aimed at making migration more difficult or less rewarding to the individual migrants. In contrast with the two sets of policies discussed before, they can be put into operation rather quickly through simple administrative changes and they affect migration directly and immediately.

The first of these policies imposes on all foreign students the requirement that upon completion of their education they leave the country of study presumably to return home for a period of two years before they can apply for an immigrant's visa.[9] Such a regulation would reduce the rate of non-return of students which for many countries represents a serious source of loss of highly educated citizens. It would be effective because the enforced departure from the country of study would eliminate the person's employment opportunities there, increase his exposure to career opportunities at home and would give him a greater chance to become reassimilated into his own culture.

[8] This proposal was made in the report of the Ditchley Conference on the Brain Drain. See Ditchley Paper No. 13, *International Migration of Talent From and To the Developed Countires: Report of a Conference at Ditchley Park* 16-19 February, 1968 (Oxford: The Ditchley Foundation, 1968).

[9] Prepared statement by John C. Shearer, "The Brain Drain of Scientists, Engineers and Physicians from the Developing Countries into the United States," in *The Brain Drain Into the United States of Scientists, Engineers, and Physicians* Hearings, U.S. Congress, House of Representatives, Committee on Government Operations, 90th Congress, 1st session, 1967, p. 23.

Such a proposed visa regulation has many disadvantages. There is no guarantee that the students would return home after having been forced to leave the country of study. Foreign students from less-developed countries faced with this kind of visa regulation in the United States have frequently chosen to move to Canada or Western Europe to wait for the two-year period to expire before returning to the United States as immigrants. However, such practices could be avoided if *all* governments agreed to cooperate in the attainment of the law's basic intent through refusal to admit as immigrants recent graduates whose passports carry reference to the two-year visa regulation.[10]

Another disadvantage of the visa regulation arises from the fact that the issuers of the visas face the need to decide upon a student's expected final degree. Such judgments are difficult to make, especially since students' ability and willingness to pursue graduate education tend to evolve during the undergraduate experience and since in many fields of study actual work experience is an integral part of the educational process. Rigid rules concerning visas issued for final degrees determined in advance thus will produce inefficiencies and lower-quality education. Flexibility in the administration of the rules, on the other hand, will open up opportunities for the avoidance of the law's intent.

Another complication of the proposed visa regulation stems from the workings of compulsory military service. When the United States had a draft law, immigrants were liable to the draft immediately, whether or not they planned to stay permanently. But as visitors, or as students, they had time to assess opportunities in the United States before plunging in as possible draftees. The proposed visa regulation would have changed this: the advantage of holding a student visa would be offset by the certainty of a two-year wait before returning to the United States. It is not clear whether, in the presence of these calculations about the possibility of being drafted, the proposed visa regulation would have increased or decreased the brain drain to the United States as regular immigrants. Some would opt for immediate United States immigration instead of student-visa status; others would remain as students, return home (possibly to conscription there), and after two or more years, stay there. Thus the policy would, under draft-law circumstances, have been both uncertain in its effect and choice-reducing to young persons.

A second policy making it more difficult for all highly skilled persons to migrate to the higher income countries would require that these countries eliminate those provisions in their immigration laws which discriminate in favor of highly skilled persons. Assuming that these countries want to retain some limitation on the *total* flow of immigrants, they should adopt a non-discriminatory policy of granting visas on the basis of the order of application, regardless of age, color, national origin, or educational or professional attainment.

[10]Staying in Canada for two years has now become more difficult to arrange.

Such a policy probably would have the desired effect of reducing the proportion of highly skilled persons in the total immigration to an advanced country like the United States. It is also basically equitable and in the liberal tradition of western societies. However, if the annual flow were large and consisted mainly of Asians and Africans, it could threaten fundamental changes in the racial, ethnic, and cultural make-up of western nations. For this reason and because most immigration laws are set with a view towards maximizing the "national interest," it is likely to be very hard to convince lawmakers to alter existing immigration policies, especially in the United States, where there has been a tradition of discriminatory legislation. The United Kingdom has already shown the strength of this kind of popular feeling. Existing political conditions leave little hope for a solution to the brain drain problem through changes in immigration laws.

A third policy which might make immigration more difficult envisages the imposition of taxes on emigrants.[11] The rationale for this tax is that it reduces the monetary income rewards accruing to emigrants and that it "compensates" the losing country for the investment it made in their education. The success of such a tax depends on its magnitude. At some arbitrarily high level it would stop all migration. What would be an efficient rate for this tax?

There is no doubt that such a tax at other than a trivial rate would reduce the magnitude of the brain drain, and that it is equitable if one believes that educated persons have an obligation towards those who paid for their education. Many problems and costs are associated with the implementation of such a tax policy. First, there is the problem of administering and enforcing it. Currently, in most western countries citizens are free to leave without encumbrance. The tax would require establishment of a new branch of the governmental bureaucracy to keep track of departing persons. This bureaucracy would collect, evaluate and act upon individuals' information about their education, the financing of this education and their intended length and the purpose of the stay abroad. The incentives and opportunities to avoid the tax through providing false information would be substantial and the the collection of the information and the taxes would require the cooperation of law enforcement officers in the country of destination. In some countries, such as the United States, where the population has complete freedom of movement and no registration requirements, it might not be easy to bring to justice foreign citizens owing tax payments to their governments, unless the tax became part of the existing set of tax treaties.

But quite apart from the difficulties of enforcement, there are the serious problems of welfare and conscience touched on in Chapter 3 in deciding what, if any, is the proper rate for this tax. If children are a consumption good, they owe society nothing for their education. If they

[11] This proposal was made in the report of the Ditchley Conference on the Brain Drain.

represent an investment good, the question becomes how much they "owe" for their education. Presumably the upper limit is set by the value of the educational services provided by the government or through philanthropy, as for example the part of the expenses of private schools covered by endowment. However, it is not realistic to argue that all of the government investment is returned to society through externalities. Probably most of the returns from education accrue to the individual and the income tax collector through the remuneration which he receives. On this view, if the tax is to be equitable and efficient it should repay society only those parts of the investment which it might regain anyway, the external benefits of education (plus perhaps, the net fiscal contribution). The measurement of these magnitudes is practically impossible.

These conceptual and measurement difficulties notwithstanding, it is always possible to set a "reasonable" tax rate by administrative fiat. But again, there exists a bewildering range of alternative methods and rates of taxation: there could be a fixed sum per emigrant or a payment proportional to the value of the educational subsidy received or tax revenue foregone. This would tend to favor the emigration of those with the greatest capital gain from emigration. On the other hand, a tax proportional to the income earned abroad, the latter on the rationale of taxation based on ability to pay, would tend to be equally inhibiting to all levels of skill. All these obligations should be adjusted for age since the older a person the more likely it will be that he has repaid his obligation to society. Such an adjustment requires the use of a discount rate for computation of the present value of the obligations and it would have to be based on precise information about the date of the person's entry into the work force and the termination of externalities; the tax might be imposed as a lump sum obligation or converted into annual payments. Easy time-payment plans would lower the effectiveness of the projected barrier.

A third serious disadvantage of a tax on highly educated emigrants is that the greater the emigrant's worldwide reputation and general ability, the easier it will be for him to have his tax paid by his foreign employer. Consequently the competition of highly educated emigrants will shift towards an average higher quality, with the result that the barrier will be the least effective for those the drained country most wishes to retain.

INTERGOVERNMENTAL COMPENSATION SCHEMES

The final policy designed to deal with the problems raised by the existence of the brain drain does so not by reducing its magnitude but by providing compensation which makes the losses less painful. This policy recommends the establishment of schemes whereby the "gaining" countries compensate "losing" countries for the value of the educational subsidy carried along by the highly educated migrants.

Such a program would be relatively simple to administer since it involves only contracts between existing governments and uses data largely already collected by immigration authorities, though such a program would provide added incentive for the collection of statistics on return migration. The setting of rates of compensation is as difficult as the setting of tax rates on individuals, with the added problem of choosing the country on which cost accounting the government subsidy is based. For example, the "value" of a Philippine nurse emigrating to the United States may at one extreme be the value of the educational subsidy in the Philippines or at the other extreme of the subsidy in the United States. Difficulties also arise in accounting for the value of the educational resources absorbed by foreign students in the country to which the immigrants come, which may or may not be used to offset the obligations incurred through the migration of fully trained persons.[12]

In spite of these difficulties, bilateral agreements can be reached, especially if the developed countries realize the value of such payments as a sign of concern for the welfare of less-developed countries, many of which consider the brain drain to involve an undesirable redistribution of world income and wealth. In the developed countries, it might be easier politically for their proponents to defend such compensation schemes, even though initially they are paid for from already appropriated foreign aid funds, than it would be to defend conventional programs of outright foreign assistance grants. Eventually, as incomes and opportunities throughout the world become equalized and improved manpower planning avoids demand and supply imbalances, the gross flows of highly educated persons will become more nearly equal and inter-country payments will balance and might ultimately cease altogether, except for a possible development on the following lines.

In the long run such compensation schemes might well lead to the extension of the principle of international specialization to the realm of human capital formation. International trade in ordinary goods and services raises world welfare because production tends to take place wherever it is relatively cheapest. Recent studies have stressed the similarity of human and physical capital both as factors of production and as users of resources currently produced but not consumed. The compensation scheme would give rise to the possibility that some countries might specialize in the production of certain types of machinery while others might specialize in the education of highly skilled persons. The machinery producers would earn foreign exchange directly, while the producers of human capital receive their payments of foreign exchange through governments.

This matter is worth dwelling on. While there are severe intellectual difficulties in deciding whether a brain drain is harming a country or not, and additional difficulties in deciding what payment would just compensate it for that harm, no one can deny that there are ways of setting up an

[12]See Chapter 10.

educational establishment as an earning enterprise that would simply by-pass these puzzles. We can see several advantages in this approach. The costs of the enterprise would determine either the compensation to be paid by a foreign government for an immigrant or the fees to be paid by a foreign student who had come for training.[13] Alternatively, the existence of a market for human capital could dictate the size of the educational establishment to be installed and maintained. This educational specialization might easily, in the long run lead to the prospering of human capital exports from the poorer, over-populated countries. It appears that most types of education are at some stage labor-intensive; this characteristic suggests that the low-wage countries would be able to offer a higher-quality product for a given compensation than could the capital-rich economies.

SUMMARY AND CONCLUSIONS

Rational policies dealing with the problem of the brain drain must be based on a clear understanding of the benefits expected from the policy and the cost which the policy would entail. Research has thus far neither produced reliable estimates of the number of persons in the brain drain flows, nor meaningful empirical measures of the welfare losses of the population in the losing countries.

In spite of the absence of reliable information on the expected net benefits from reductions in the brain drain, it is not too soon to consider the economic and social costs of policies aimed at the reduction of the flows. Policies which attempt to do so by narrowing income and opportunity gaps among nations are universally desirable on many grounds other than their effect on the brain drain. Their disadvantage lies exclusively in the long period required for them to become effective.

Policies designed to make migration more difficult, whether through changes in national laws on immigration and student visas or through the imposition of taxes on emigrants, appear to be unrealistic from a political point of view. They are also likely to result in inefficiencies, and to involve very high costs of administration and the loss of personal freedom.

The proposal for the institution of intergovernmental compensation schemes for the repayment of educational subsidies invested in the emigrants by the losing country appears to have the greatest merits and least social cost. Its long-term beneficial effects may be very great through its influence on international trade, it is especially acceptable to those who

[13] It might occur to some that it would also be possible to generalize this approach and let the emigrant (or his parents) pay the compensation. We agree. But we are brought back to our conceptual puzzles of Chapter 3: Why should a father who has in effect already paid through taxes for his son's education, pay again to "compensate" the state for that son's emigration? Should the state now compensate the taxpayers? That the idea is absurd reinforces our belief that "debt" and "compensation" are not helpful ideas for understanding the real gains and losses associated with the brain drain.

believe that the brain drain results in an undesirable redistribution of world wealth and income, and it can be put into effect with a minimum of administrative effort.

Given the existing state of knowledge about the magnitude of the welfare losses resulting from the brain drain, the foregoing analysis suggests, in the judgment of the authors, that the first set of policies designed to narrow income and opportunity gaps throughout the world are highly desirable. Intergovernmental compensation schemes similarly can be expected to increase world welfare. On the other hand, the social cost of making migration and foreign study more difficult or less rewarding appears to be greater than the social benefits to be gained by the cure of the brain drain.

A SELECTED BIBLIOGRAPHY ON THE BRAIN DRAIN, GENERAL MIGRATION AND HUMAN CAPITAL

PART I: PUBLICATIONS IDENTIFIABLE BY INDIVIDUAL AUTHOR

Abraham, P.M. "Regaining High Level Indian Manpower from Abroad—A Review of Policies, Programs and Problems." *Manpower Journal* 3 (1968): 83-117.

Adams, Walter, ed. *The Brain Drain*. New York: Macmillan, 1968.

Aitken, N. D. "The International Flow of Human Capital: Comment." *American Economic Review* 58 (1968): 539-545.

Bachmura, Frank T. "Latin American Brain Drainage." Department of Economics, Indiana University (mimeo).

Barkin, Solomon. "The Economic Costs and Benefits and Human Gains and Disadvantages of International Migration." *Journal of Human Resources* 2 (1967): 495-516.

Becker, Gary. *Human Capital*. New York: National Bureau of Economic Research, Columbia University Press, 1964.

Benham,L.; Maurizi, A.; and Reder, M. W. "Migration, Location and Remuneration of Medical Personnel: Physicians and Dentists." *Review of Economics and Statistics* 50 (1968): 332-347.

Berry, Albert and Soligo, Ronald. "Some Welfare Aspects of International Migration." *Journal of Political Economy* 77 (1969): 778-794.

Bhagwati, J. and Dellalfar, W. "The Brain Drain and Income Taxation." *World Development* 1, 1 & 2 (1973).

Bhagwati, J. N. and Martington, M. eds. *Taxing the Brain: A Proposal*. Vols. 1 & 2. Amsterdam: North Holland Publishing Co., 1976.

Blank, David M., and Stigler, George J. *The Demand and Supply of Scientific Personnel*. New York: National Bureau of Economic Research Inc., 1957.

Blaug, M., ed. *Economics of Education 1 and 2*. London: Penguin Modern Economics, 1968.

———. "Optimal Wage and Education Policy with International Migration" (mimeo).

———."Approaches to Educational Planning." *Economic Journal* 77, 306 (June 1967).

Blaug, M.; Layard, P.R.G.: Woodhall, M. *The Causes of Graduate Unemployment in India*. London: Alain Lane, 1969.

Blume, Stuart. " 'Brain Drain'—A Look at the Literature." *Universities Quarterly* (1968): 281-290.

Bowman, M.J. and Myers, R. G. "Schooling, Experience and Gains and Losses in Human Capital Through Migration." *Journal of the American Statistical Association* 62 (1967): 875-898.

Butterfield, Herbert. *The Origins of Modern Science*. New York: Macmillan, 1960.

Comay, Yochanon. "The Benefits and Costs of Study Abroad and Migration." *Canadian Journal of Economics* 3 (1970).

________. "Migration of Professional Manpower Between Canada and the United States." Princeton University: Department of Economics, 1969 (mimeo).

Crane, Robert J. "Technical Education and Economic Development in India before World War I." In C. A. Anderson and M. J. Bowman. *Education and Economic Development*. Chicago: University of Chicago Press, 1967.

Dales, J. H. "Canadian Scholarship in Economics: Achievement and Outlook." An address to the Royal Society of Canada, 7 June 1967.

Dampier, W.C. *A Shorter History of Science*. New York: Meridian, 1957.

Dedijer, Stevan. "Why did Daedalus Leave?" *Science*, June 30, 1961.

________. "'Modern' Migration," In W. Adams, ed. *The Brain Drain*. New York: Macmillan, 1968.

________. "Underdeveloped Science in Underdeveloped Countries." *Minerva* 2 (1963): 61-81.

________. "Migration of Scientists." *Nature* (March 7, 1964): 964-967.

Fein, Rashi. "Education Patterns in Southern Migration." *Southern Economic Journal* 32 (1965): 106-124.

Fortney, Judith A. "International Migration of Professionals." *Population Studies* 24 (1970): 217-232.

Friborg, Göran. "Report of the Committee for Scientific and Technical Personnel, International Movement of Scientific and Technical Personnel." Paris: OECD, August 1965 (mimeo).

________. "International Movement of Scientific and Technical Personnel." Stockholm: Committee on Research Economics, Swedish Research Council, December, 1966.

________. "A First, Preliminary Report ... Regarding the Migration of Scientists to and from Sweden." Stockholm: Swedish Research Council Committee on Research Economics, 1968. Report No. 20 (mimeo).

________. *Brain Drain Statistics: Empirical Evidence and Guidelines*. Stockholm: Swedish Research Council Committee on Research Economics, 1975. Report 6.

________. *Motives and Qualifications of Scientists and Engineers Emigrated from Sweden to the U.S.A.* Stockholm: Committee on Research Economics. Swedish Research Council, Report No. 39, 1969.

________. "The Migration of Scientists—A Case Study." *TVF* 36 (1965).

Gilbert, Abraham-Frois. "Population, Human Capital and International Migrations." *Revue d'Economie Appliquè* 74 (1964): 526-559.

Gollin, Albert, ed. *The International Migration of Talent and Skills, Proceedings of a Workshop*. Washington: U.S. Department of State, Department of International Educational and Cultural Affairs, October, 1966.

Greenwood, David. *Scientific Manpower from Abroad—United States Scientists and Engineers of Foreign Birth and Training*. N.S.F. Publication. Washington, USG PO (1962): 62-24.

Grubel, H. G. "Nonreturning Foreign Students and the Cost of Student Exchange." *International Educational and Cultural Exchange*. Publication of the U.S. Advisory Commission on International Educational and Cultural Affairs, 1966.

———. "The Brain Drain: A U.S. Dilemma." *Science* 154 (16 December 1966): 1420-1423.

———. "Foreign Manpower in U.S. Sciences." *Review of Income and Wealth* (1968).

———. "The Reduction of the Brain Drain: Problems and Policies." *Minerva* (1968).

———. *Characteristics of Foreign Born and Educated Scientists in the United States 1966*. Distributed by the National Science Foundation, Washington, 1969.

———. "Some Empirical Measures of the Brain Drain." In R. McGinn's, ed., volume on Human Mobility, to be published by Cornell University Press, 1971.

———. "Foreign Scientists in the United States." *Bulletin of the Atomic Scientists* (February 1970).

Grubel, H. G. and M. B. McAlpin. "Austrian, German and Swiss Economists in the United States." *Kyklos* 21 (1968): 299-312.

Grubel, H. G. and Scott, A. D. "The International Flow of Human Capital." *American Economic Review* 56 (1966): 268-274.

Grubel, H. G. and Scott, A. D. "Foreigners in the U.S. Economics Profession." *American Economic Review* 57, 1 (March 1967): 131-145.

Grubel, H. G. and Scott, A. D. "The International Flow of Human Capital: Reply." *American Economic Review* 58 (1968): 539-548.

Grubel, H. G. and Scott, A. D. "The Immigration of Scientists and Engineers to the United States 1949-61." *Journal of Political Economy* 74 (1966): 368-378.

Grubel, H. G. and Scott, A. D. "The Cost of U.S. College Student Exchange Programs." *The Journal of Human Resources* 1 (1966): 81-98.

Grubel, H. G. and Scott, A. D. "The Characteristics of Foreigners in the U.S. Economics Profession." *American Economic Review* 5 (1967): 127-139.

Grubel, H. G. and Scott, A. D. "Determinants of Migration: The Highly Skilled." *International Migration* 5, 2 (1967).

Grubel, H. G. and Scott, A. D. "The International Movement of Human Capital: Canadian Economists." *Canadian Journal of Economics* 2 (1969): 375-388.

Gupta, Suraj. "The Economics of International Migration—A Theoretical Analysis." Department of Economics, University of Western Ontario, 1965 (mimeo).

Halpern, Burton M. "New Exodus, Israel's Talent Drain." *The Nation* (May 1965).

Harberger, A. C. "Using the Resources at Hand More Effectively." *American Economic Review* 49 (May 1954): 134-146.

Harris, S. E. *Higher Education: Resources and Finance.* New York: McGraw-Hill, 1962.

Henderson, Gregory. "Foreign Students: Exchange or Immigration?" *Foreign Service Journal* (April 1965).

Henry, D. "University Problems in Recruitment of Teaching and Research Personnel from Abroad." *The Educational Record* (Winter, 1967).

Horowitz, Morris A. *La Emigracien de Profesionales Y Technicos Argentinos.* Editorial del Instituto, Buenos Aires, 1962.

Hunt, Halsey G. "The Brain Drain in Medicine." *Federation Bulletin* of the Federation of State Medical Boards of the United States 53 (1966): 98-107.

Isaac, J. *Economics of Migration*. London: Kegan Paul, 1947.

Johnson, Harry G. "The Economics of the Brain Drain: The Canadian Case." *Minerva* 3 (1965): 306.

________. "The International Circulation of Human Capital: Comments on Thomas's Analysis of Brain Drain." *Minerva* 6 (1967): 105-110.

________. "The Economic Theory of Customs Union." *Pakistan Economic Journal* 10 (March 1960): 14-32.

________. "Canadian Contributions to the Discipline of Economics Since 1945." *Canadian Journal of Economics* 1, 1 (February 1968): 129-146.

________. "The Social Sciences in the Age of Opulence." *Canadian Journal of Economics and Political Science* 32, 4 (November 1966): 423-442.

________. "Some Economic Aspects of the Brain Drain." *Pakistan Development Review* 7 (Autumn 1967): 379-411.

________. "Notes on the Effects of Emigration of Professional People on the Welfare of those Remaining Behind" (mimeo).

Kannappan, Subbiah. "The Brain Drain and Developing Countries." *International Labour Review* 48 (1968): 1-26.

Kelly, P. J. and Nicholls, N. M. "The Migration of Scientists to and from Australia—A Quantitative Survey, 1961-67." *The Australian Journal of Science* 32 (1969).

Kidd, Charles V. "The Growth of Scientists and the Distribution of Scientists among Nations." *Impact*. UNESCO 14 (1964).

________. "The Brain Drain of Scientists, Engineers and Physicians from the Developing Countries to the United States." *The Brain Drain Into the United States of Scientists, Engineers, and Physicians* Hearings,

U.S. Congress, House of Representatives, Committee on Government Operations, 90th Congress, 1st session, 1967.

———. "The Economics of the Brain Drain." *Minerva* 2 (1965).

Kindleberger, Charles. "Emigration and Economic Growth." *Banca Nazionale del Lavoro Quarterly Review* 18 (Sept. 1965): 234-254.

Last, J. M. "International Mobility in the Medical Profession." In Bechhofer, F., ed. *Population Growth and the Brain Drain*. Edinburgh: University Press, 1969.

Mackay, D. I. *Geographical Mobility and the Brain Drain: A Case Study of Aberdeen University Graduates, 1860-1960*. London: George Allen & Unwin, Ltd., 1969.

Markowitz, H. *Portfolio Selection*. Cowles Foundation Monograph 16. New York: Wiley, 1959.

Myers, C. A. and Harbison, F. *Education, Manpower and Economic Growth*. New York: McGraw-Hill, 1963.

Myers, Charles A. "The Importance of Higher Education to Development." *Higher Education and the International Flow of Manpower: Implications for the Developing World*. University of Minnesota, 1967.

Myers, R. G. "Study Abroad and the Migration of Human Resources." Ph.D. thesis, University of Chicago, 1967.

Myers, Robert C. "Brain Drains and Brain Gains." *International Development Review* 9 (1967): 4-9.

Michalopoulos, Constantine. "Labor Migration and Optimum Population." *Kyklos* 21 (1968): 130-143.

Mishan, E. J. "The Brain Drain: Why Worry So Much?" *New Society* (November 2, 1967): 619-622.

Naficy, Habib. "The 'Brain Drain': The Case of Iranian Non-Returnees." Embassy of Iran, Washington, D.C. (A report presented at the annual conference of the Society for International Development, New York City, March 17, 1966).

Olivier, Michel. "Algerians, Africans and Frenchmen." *Interplay* 1 (May 1968): 20-25.

Parai, Louis. *Immigration and Emigration of Professional and Skilled Manpower During the Post-War Period*. Special Study No. 1, Economic Council of Canada. Ottawa: Queen's Printer, 1965.

Pankhurst, K. V. "Migration Between Canada and the United States." *Annals of the American Academy of Political and Social Science* 367 (1966).

Payne, G. L. *Britain's Scientific and Technological Manpower*. Stanford: Stanford University Press, 1960.

Perkins, James A. "Foreign Aid and the Brain Drain." *Foreign Affairs* (July 1966).

Preston, R. A. "Two-Way Traffic in Canadian History." *Queen's Quarterly* 74 (Autumn 1967).

Psacharopoulos, George (with Hinchliffe, K.). *Returns to Education: An International Comparison*. Amsterdam: Elsevier Scientific Publishing Company, 1973.

Reder, Melvin W. "The Economic Consequences of Increased Immigration." *Review of Economics and Statistics* 45 (1963).

Rostow, W. W. *The Stages of Economic Growth*. Cambridge, 1960.

Russett, B. *et al*. *World Handbook of Political and Social Indicators*. New Haven: Yale University Press, 1964.

Samuel, T. J. *Migration of Canadian-Born Between Canada and United States of America, 1955 to 1968*. Ottawa: Research Branch, Program Development Service, Department of Manpower and Immigration, 1969.

Salam, Abdus. "The Isolation of the Scientist in Developing Countries." *Minerva* 4 (1966).

Schultz, Theodore W. "Capital Formation by Education." *Journal of Political Economy* 68 (1960): 571-583.

________. "Value of U.S. Farm Surpluses to Underdeveloped Countries." *Journal of Farm Economics* (December 1960).

________. "Reflections on Investment in Man." *Journal of Political Economy*, Supplement 70 (1962).

________. "Education and Economic Growth." In Nelson B. Henry, ed. *Social Forces Influencing American Education*. Chicago: National Society for the Study of Education, 1961. 46-88.

________. *The Economic Value of Education*. New York: Columbia University Press, 1963.

Scott, A. D. "The Recruitment and Migration of Canadian Social Scientists." *Canadian Journal of Economics and Political Science* 33 (Nov. 1967): 495-508.

________. "The International Circulation of Human Capital: Comments on Thomas's Analysis of Brain Drain." *Minerva* 6 (1967): 110-116.

Seers, Dudley. "The Brain Drain from Poor Countries." Communications Series 31, Institute of Development Studies, University of Sussex (mimeo).

Sheffield, Edward and McGrail, Mary Margo, eds. "The Retrieval of Canadian Graduate Students from Abroad." Ottawa: Association of Universities and Colleges of Canada, 1966.

Shearer, John C. "The Brain Drain of Scientists, Engineers and Physicians from the Developing Countries to the United States." *The Brain Drain Into the United States of Scientists, Engineers, and Physicians* Hearings, U.S. Congress, House of Representatives, Committee on Government Operations, 90th Congress, 1st session, 1967.

Sjaastad, L. "The Costs and Returns of Human Migration." *Journal of Political Economy*, Part 2, Supplement 70 (1962).

Smiley, D. "Contributions to Canadian Political Science since the Second

World War." *Canadian Journal of Economics and Political Science* 33, 4 (November 1967): 569-580.

Susskind, Charles and Schell, Lynn. *Berkeley—Golden Gate for Foreign Engineers*. Berkeley: Institute of International Studies, University of California, March, 1967 (draft).

Taylor, K. W. "Economic Scholarship in Canada." *Canadian Journal of Economics and Political Science* 26, 1 (1960).

Timlin, Mable. "Social Science Research in Canada." In Faucher, A. and Timlin, M. *Social Sciences in Canada*. Ottawa, 1968.

Thomas, Brinley, ed. *Economics of International Migration*. London: Macmillan, 1958.

———. *International Migration and Economic Development: A Trend Report and Bibliography*. Paris: United Nations Educational, Scientific, and Cultural Organization, 1961: 65-85.

———. "The International Circulation of Human Capital." *Minerva* 5 (Summer 1967): 479-504.

———. "Reply to Correspondence." *Minerva* 6 (1968): 423-427.

Tobin, J. "Liquidity Preference as Behavior Towards Risk." *Review of Economic Studies* (February 1958).

Weisbrod, B. *External Benefits of Public Education: An Economic Analysis*. Princeton: Princeton University Press, 1964.

West, E. G. "Welfare Economics and Emigration Taxes." *Southern Economic Journal* 36 (1969): 52-59.

West, K. M. "Foreign Interns and Residents in the United States." *Journal of Medical Education* 40 (December, 1965).

———. "Migration of Latin American Physicians to the United States." A report presented to the Advisory Committee on Medical Research of the Pan American Health Organization, May 1966 (preliminary draft).

West, M. "Training for Medical Research: The World Role of the United States." *The Journal of Medical Education* (March 1964).

Wilkinson, B. W. *Studies on the Economics of Education*. Occasional Paper No. 4, Economics and Research Branch, Department of Labour, Ottawa, July 1965.

Wilson, James A. "The Emigration of British Scientists." *Minerva* 5 (1966): 20-29.

PART II: PUBLICATIONS BY INTERNATIONAL AND NATIONAL OFFICIAL AGENCIES

American Academy of Political and Social Science. "The New Immigration." *Annals* of the American Academy of Political and Social Science 367 (September, 1966). Entire issue.

Canada, Department of Labour, Economics and Statistics Branch. "The Migration of Professional Workers into and out of Canada, 1946-1960." *Professional Manpower Bulletin*, No. 11 (October 1961).

Canada, Department of Labour, Economics and Research Branch. "After-Graduation Plans of Final-Year Students in Engineering and Science Courses, 1958-1963." *Professional Manpower Bulletin*, PM/5 (May 1964).

________. "Survey of Canadians Enrolled at American Universities and Colleges, 1962-3." *Professional Manpower Bulletin*, PM/4 (February 1964).

Ditchley Paper No. 13. *International Migration of Talent from and to the Less-Developed Countries: Report of a Conference at Ditchley Park, 16-19 February, 1968*. Oxford: The Ditchley Foundation, 1968.

Institute of International Education, Committee on Educational Interchange Policy. *The Foreign Student: Exchange or Immigrant?* New York, 1958.

Inter-Agency Task Force of the Council on International and Cultural Affairs. *The Problem of the Non-Returning Exchange Visitor*. CEC Paper No. 10, April 23, 1965. Distributed by the Bureau of Educational and Cultural Affairs, Department of State, Washington, D.C.

International Labour Organization, U.N. *International Migration, 1945-57*. Geneva, 1959.

Organization for Economic Cooperation and Development, Committee for Scientific and Technical Personnel. *International Movement of Scientific and Technical Personnel*. Paris, 1965 (mimeo).

________. "The Utilization of Highly Qualified Personnel." Venice Conference 25th to 27th October 1971. Paris, 1973.

Pan American Health Organization. *Migration of Health Personnel, Scientists and Engineers from Latin America*. Scientific Publication 142. Washington, D.C., September, 1966, p. 12.

United Kingdom. *Emigration of Scientists from the United Kingdom*. Report of a Committee Appointed by the Council of the Royal Society (The Sutherland Committee). London: The Royal Society, Burlington House, Picadilly, February 1963. Summarized in *Minerva* 2 (1963).

United Kingdom, Committee on Manpower Resources for Science and Technology. *The Brain Drain: Report of the Working Group on Migration*. London: HMSO, Cmnd. 3417, 1967.

United Nations, Report of the Secretary General. "Outflow of Trained Personnel from Developing Countries." A/7294, November, 1968.

United Nations, Conference on Trade and Development. "The Reverse Transfer of Technology: Economic Effects of the Outflow of Trained Personnel from Developing Countries." Geneva: UNCTAD Trade and Development Board, July 15, 1974. GE74-45088 (mimeo).

United Nations, Report of the Secretary General. "Outflow of Trained Personnel from Developing to Developed Countries." E/C. 8/21. New York, 1974.

United States, National Academy of Sciences. *Doctorate Production in U.S. Universities, 1920-62*. 1963.

United States, National Academy of Sciences, National Research Council. *Doctorate Production in the United States Universities, 1936-56*. Washington, D.C.: National Academy of Sciences National Research Council, 1958.

United States, National Science Foundation. *Immigration of Professional Workers to the United States—1953-56*. Scientific Manpower Bulletin No. 8. Washington, D.C., February 1958.

________. *Scientific Manpower from Abroad*. United States Scientists and Engineers of Foreign Birth and Training. NSF 62-24.

U. S. Government. *The Brain Drain of Scientists, Engineers and Physicians from the Developing Countries into the United States: Hearings Before a Subcommittee of the Committee on Government Operations, House of Representatives*. Washington: U.S. Government Printing Office, 1968.

________. *Scientific Brain Drain from the Developing Countries: Twenty-third Report by the Committee on Government Operations*. Washington: U.S. Government Printing Office, 1968.

United States. *The Brain Drain into the United States of Scientists, Engineers, and Physicians*. Staff Study for the Research and Technical Programs Subcommittee of the Committee on Government Operations, U.S. Congress. Washington, 1967.

PART III: OTHER BIBLIOGRAPHIES ON THE BRAIN DRAIN

Dedijer, S. and Svenningson, L. *Brain Drain and Brain Gain: A Bibliography on Migration of Scientists, Engineers, Doctors and Students*. Lund, Sweden: Research Policy Program, 1967.

Parker, Franklin. "Government Policy and International Education: A Selected and Partially Annotated Bibliography." In Stewart Fraser (ed.), *Government Policy and International Education*. New York: Wiley, 1965.

Scheurer, W. G.; Shearer, John C.; *et al.* "Selected Bibliography International Movement of High-Level Human Resources (The 'Brain Drain') by Sender Area." Pennsylvania State University and University of Chicago Comparative Education Center, May 1967 (mimeo).

Schwicliff, A. W. *Publications and Research Related to the International Migration of Professional Manpower*. Washington: Education and World Affairs, 1967 (mimeo).